DOGECOIN

HISTORY OF THE FIRST YEAR

A DECENTRALISED CRYPTOCURRENCY
PART OF THE "ALT-ERNATIVE" BOOK SERIES

Dogecoin—History of the First Year

by Christopher P. Thompson

Book Author by Christopher P. Thompson

Book Design by C. Ellis

ISBN—13: 978-1519667359

ISBN—10: 1519667353

DOGECOIN

HISTORY OF THE FIRST YEAR

A DECENTRALISED CRYPTOCURRENCY
PART OF THE "ALT-ERNATIVE" BOOK SERIES

CHRISTOPHER P. THOMPSON

ABOUT THE AUTHOR

Christopher Paul Thompson is an avid cryptocurrency enthusiast from the United Kingdom. Born in Bradford, UK and academically educated at the University of York (BSc Mathematics). He has been a keen follower of past and current events in the crypto space since March 2013. His first book called Cryptocurrency "The Alt-ernative" A Beginner's Reference is the first book he has ever written.

Other titles currently available:

"Peercoin—History of the First Year"

"Reddcoin—History of the First Year"

"DigiByte—History of the First Year"

Other titles planned for release are:

"Quark—History of the First Year"

"Dash—History of the First Year"

"Cryptographic Decentralised
Currencies and Assets—
The "Alt-ernative" Book"

E-mail Contact: chris_thompson25@live.co.uk
Twitter Contact: https://twitter.com/MrSilverCider

CONTENTS

CONTENTS

INTRODUCTION

Cryptocurrency was born with the advent of Bitcoin. It was first mentioned in a research paper published online titled "Bitcoin: A Peer-to-Peer Electronic Cash System" with the real name or pseudonym Satoshi Nakamoto attributed to it. This paper was published on the 31st of October 2008. About two months later on the 3rd of January 2009, the Bitcoin network protocol was launched. This technological breakthrough was the beginning of a decentralized public ledger. It allows people to send value across the globe without the permission of a third party authority.

Since then, a growing number of people around the world have been introduced to or discovered cryptocurrency. Many cryptocurrencies have been launched over the following years since the introduction of Bitcoin. The name "alternative" was given to these cryptocurrencies after Bitcoin because they were introduced, implemented and developed to be used instead of or alongside Bitcoin. One could say, a choice of brand in cryptocurrency exists. People have discovered these either through word of mouth, by accident, through personal investigation or via the media. Nevertheless, it has changed the lives of many people. It has provoked the general public into asking innumerable questions about many issues based on subjects such as economics, politics, philosophy, mathematics and so on.

In this book, I hope to give the reader insight into how one particular alternative cryptocurrency began. Dogecoin began in late 2013 as a Scrypt proof of work clone of Luckycoin. This book, as well as other future books to be written on other cryptocurrencies, is a historical story of the first year. It covers the time from the initial announcement on Bitcointalk up until the blockchain had been publicly available for one year. In this case, from the 8th of December 2013 to the 8th of December 2014. It also describes the terminology one encounters in cryptocurrency such as proof of work mining, block reward, wallets and so on.

INTRODUCTION

I chose to write about just the first year for various reasons, some of which are:

- For almost all cryptocurrencies, the first year of their existence is the most defining period.

- If I had chosen to write a full history of Dogecoin, I would be continuously playing catch up.

- Most other cryptocurrencies are not several years old yet, so I have limited the scope of all books on individual cryptocurrencies at this time.

- Currently I have a full-time job besides being a cryptocurrency author, so my time is unfortunately limited.

You may have bought this book because Dogecoin is your favourite cryptocurrency. Alternatively, you may be keen to find out how it all began. I have presented the information henceforth without going into too much technical discussion about Dogecoin. If you would like to investigate further, I recommended that you read material currently available online at the official website at www.dogecoin.com. Also, the official subreddit at https://www.reddit.com/r/dogecoin has masses of information via which one can contact some of those people involved in the development of Dogecoin.

If you choose to purchase a certain amount of Dogecoin, please do not buy more than you can afford to lose.

Enjoy the book :D

WHAT IS DOGECOIN?

Dogecoin is a cryptocurrency or digital decentralised currency used via the Internet featuring the image of a Shiba Inu Dog from the "Doge" meme of the year 2013. It is described as a payment network without the need for a central authority such as a bank or other central clearing house. It allows the end user to store or transfer value anywhere in the world with the use of a personal computer, laptop or smartphone (mobile/cellphone). Cryptography has been implemented and coded into the network allowing the user to send currency through a decentralised (no centre point of failure), open source (anyone can review the code), peer-to-peer network. Cryptography also controls the creation of newly mined Dogecoin units of account, DOGE.

Billy Markus (a programmer from Oregon, USA) and Jack Palmer (Adobe marketing specialist from Sydney, Australia) were the co-founders of the coin. It was Billy Markus who derived Dogecoin from the source code of Luckycoin, a Scrypt based coin with random block rewards. Both co-founders initially treated the project as a "joke" so never thought it would become very popular in the cryptocurrency space.

During the first year, Dogecoin was used as a means to raise money for worthwhile causes. Most notably, funds were raised to help the Jamaican Bobsleigh Team reach the Sochi Olympic Games and to sponsor Nascar driver Josh Wise. Besides other fundraisers, the generosity and drive of the community promoted the coin. It has since become one of the most active cryptocurrenices in existence today.

Members of the community usually say "To the moon!" to celebrate its rise in monetary value. The slogan used by the Dogecoin community to market the coin is:

"THE FUN AND FRIENDLY
INTERNET CURRENCY"

WHY USE DOGECOIN?

Like all cryptocurrencies, people have chosen to adopt Dogecoin as a medium of exchange through personal choice. An innovative feature of the coin, an affinity towards the brand or high confidence of the community could be reasons why they have done so. Key benefits of using Dogecoin are:

- It is a useful medium of exchange via which value can be transferred anywhere in the world for a fraction of the cost of other conventional methods such as Western Union.

- Dogecoin eliminates the need for a trusted third party such as a bank, clearing house or other centralised authority (e.g. PayPal). All transactions are solely from one person to another (peer-to-peer).

- Dogecoin has the potential to engage people worldwide who are without a bank account (unbanked).

- Dogecoin transactions are irreversible by design.

- Dogecoin is immune from the effects of hyperinflation, unlike the current fiat monetary systems around the world.

Thanks to Josh Mohland and David Dvorak, the DogeTipBot was created on Reddit on the 15th of December 2013. It is a service which allows users to send DOGE to others. Therefore, the coin is used to tip great content, show appreciation or donate to a worthwhile cause. From the 15th of December 2013 to the 5th of December 2014, the following were the case:

- Over 735,000 completed (accepted) tips were processed.

- About 75,000 users signed up to DogeTipBot.

- A mean transaction size of roughly $0.03 (60 DOGE).

IS DOGECOIN MONEY?

Money is a form of acceptable, convenient and valued medium of payment for goods and services within an economy. It allows two parties to exchange goods or services without the need to barter. This eradicates the potential situation where one party of the two may not want what the other has to offer. The main properties of money are:

- **As a medium of exchange**—money can be used as a means to buy/sell goods/services without the need to barter.

- **A unit of account**—a common measure of value wherever one is in the world.

- **Portable**—easily transferred from one party to another. The medium used can be easily carried.

- **Durable**—all units of the currency can be lost, but not destroyed.

- **Divisible**—each unit can be subdivided into smaller fractions of that unit.

- **Fungible**— each unit of account is the same as every other unit within the medium (1 DOGE = 1 DOGE)

- **As a store of value**—it sustains its purchasing power (what it can buy) over long periods of time.

Dogecoin easily satisfies the first six characteristics. Taking into account the last characteristic, the value of Dogecoin, like all currencies, comes from people willing to accept it as a medium of exchange for payment of goods or services. As it gets adopted by more individuals or merchants, its intrinsic value will increase accordingly.

DOGECOIN SPECIFICATION

Since the birth of Dogecoin, its coin specification has changed a few times. At the time of publication of this book, its current specification is:

Coin Symbol:	Đ
Unit of account:	DOGE
Date of Announcement:	8th of December 2013 03:55:25 UTC
Genesis Block Generated:	None
Block Number One Generated:	8th of December 2013 03:55:27 UTC
Date of Launch:	8th of December 2013 03:55:27 UTC
Founders:	Jack Palmer and Billy Markus
Lead Developer:	Max Keller
Hashing Algorithm:	Scrypt
Timestamping Algorithm:	Auxiliary Proof of Work
Address Begins With:	D
Total Coins:	No limit (see block distribution table)
Block Time:	60 seconds
Difficulty Retarget Time:	60 seconds (DigiShield)
Coins per Block:	10,000 DOGE
Confirmations per Transaction:	6
Pre-mine:	None

DOGECOIN MILESTONE TIMELINE

8th of December 2013	—Dogecoin announced on Bitcointalk.org
8th of December 2013	—First block mined at 03:55:27 UTC
8th of December 2013	—/r/dogecoin created at 12:36:11 UTC.
8th of December 2013	—First Dogecoin forum created at www.doges.org.
8th of December 2013	—Official @dogecoin Twitter page created.
11th of December 2013	—Current Dogecoin logo published.
12th of December 2013	—Coined Up was the first exchange to trade DOGE.
12th of December 2013	—Version 1.1 of the wallet client released.
14th of December 2013	—Market capitalisation surpassed $1 million.
15th of December 2013	—Dogecoin added to www.coinmarketcap.com.
18th of December 2013	—Cryptsy was the second exchange to trade DOGE.
18th of December 2013	—Version 1.2 of the wallet client released.
19th of December 2013	—Coins-e was the third exchange to trade DOGE.
20th of December 2013	—Number of DOGE mined surpassed 10 billion.
20th of December 2013	—An exchange called Vircurex added Dogecoin.
23rd of December 2013	—An exchange called Bter added Dogecoin.
25th of December 2013	—An exchange called CoinEx added Dogecoin.
26th of December 2013	—Version 1.3 of the wallet client released.
29th of December 2013	—The official Facebook group was created.
1st of January 2014	—An exchange called BTC-8 added Dogecoin.
5th of January 2014	—Version 1.4 of the wallet client released.
8th of January 2014	—AltQuick.co introduced direct USD purchase of DOGE.
8th of January 2014	—An exchange called OpenEx added Dogecoin.
18th of January 2014	—Version 1.4.1 of the wallet client released.
18th of January 2014	—An exchange called C-Cex added Dogecoin.
20th of January 2014	—Over $30,000 raised for the Jamaican Bobsled Team.

DOGECOIN MILESTONE TIMELINE

21st of January 2014	—Market capitalisation surpassed $50 million.
22nd of January 2014	—An exchange called Poloniex added Dogecoin.
28th of January 2014	—Version 1.5 of the wallet client released.
29th of January 2014	—An exchange called Vault of Satoshi added Dogecoin.
1st of February 2014	—An exchange called Swisscex added Dogecoin.
2nd of February 2014	—Dogecoin not capped at 100 billion!!
6th of February 2014	—Doge4kids successfully raised 20 million DOGE.
8th of February 2014	—Version 1.5.1 of the wallet client released.
11th of February 2014	—An exchange called BTC38 added Dogecoin.
11th of February 2014	—An exchange called Newaltex added Dogecoin.
12th of February 2014	—All time high market capitalisation of 2014 reached.
14th of February 2014	—First reduction in the block reward at 03:00:22 UTC.
17th of February 2014	—Version 1.5.2 of the wallet client released.
19th of February 2014	—An exchange called MintPal added Dogecoin.
20th of February 2014	—An exchange called Kraken added Dogecoin.
20th of February 2014	—An exchange called Comkort added Dogecoin.
4th of March 2014	—Doge4water charity campaign initiated.
12th of March 2014	—Version 1.6 of the wallet client released.
14th of March 2014	—An exchange called Coin Market added Dogecoin.
15th of March 2014	—An exchange called AGX.io added Dogecoin.
16th of March 2014	—Doge4water successfully raised 40 million DOGE.
17th of March 2014	—Fixed block reward of 250,000 DOGE began.
20th of March 2014	—Sponsorship of Nascar driver (#98) Josh Wise began.
25th of March 2014	—67.8 million (~$55,000) DOGE raised for Josh Wise.
26th of March 2014	—Dogecoin attended CoinSummit in San Francisco.

DOGECOIN MILESTONE TIMELINE

1st of April 2014	—Dogecoin went live on GoCoin (payment processor)
3rd of April 2014	—"Dogecoin Core 1.7 Alpha" wallet client released.
6th of April 2014	—Charlie Lee proposed merged mining.
12th of April 2014	—"Dogecoin 1.7.0 Beta 1" wallet client released.
16th of April 2014	—Announcement of conference in San Francisco.
17th of April 2014	—An exchange called BTC100 added Dogecoin.
17th of April 2014	—First issue of the Dogecoin Magazine published.
22nd of April 2014	—"Dogecoin 1.7.0 Beta 2" wallet client released.
25th of April 2014	—Dogecoin conference held in San Francisco.
28th of April 2014	—Second reduction in the block reward.
1st of May 2014	—Doge4Housing achieved goal of 11 million DOGE.
4th of May 2014	—Josh Wise finished 20th at Talledega in Alabama, USA.
4th of May 2014	—"Dogecoin 1.7.0 RC-1" wallet client released.
7th of May 2014	—Original Dogecoin Foundation dismantled.
12th of May 2014	—Version 1.7.0 of the Dogecoin wallet client released.
13th of May 2014	—An exchange called CoinNext added Dogecoin.
16th of May 2014	—Josh Wise won the "Sprint Fan Vote".
17th of May 2014	—Josh Wise finished 15th at Charlotte in N Carolina.
3rd of June 2014	—An exchange called HitBTC added Dogecoin.
4th of June 2014	—An exchange called Kingcoiny added Dogecoin.
6th of June 2014	—Facebook approved the "Doge Tipping App".
8th of June 2014	—An exchange called mcxNOW added Dogecoin.
14th of June 2014	—3 million DOGE were successfully raised for CESHEO.
15th of June 2014	—Version 1.7.1 of the Dogecoin wallet client released.
24th of June 2014	—Jack Palmer unsubscribed from /r/Dogecoin.
25th of June 2014	—Official Dogecoin Foundation Twitter Page created.

DOGECOIN MILESTONE TIMELINE

1st of July 2014	—New Dogecoin Foundation established.
15th of July 2014	—Third reduction in the block reward.
30th of July 2014	—Tristan Winters interviewed 'langerhans'.
3rd of August 2014	—Developers decided to go ahead with merge mining.
13th of August 2014	—Dogeparty Bitcointalk thread created.
15th of August 2014	—Jason Calacanis interviewed Josh Mohland.
20th of August 2014	—An exchange called CEX.IO added Dogecoin.
24th of August 2014	—Version 1.8 of the Dogecoin wallet client released.
3rd of September 2014	—CheapAir.com add Dogecoin as a method of payment.
11th of September 2014	—AuxPoW began at block number 371,337.
11th of September 2014	—2.5 million DOGE raised for Doge4Kashmir.
18th of September 2014	—An exchange called Cryptonit added Dogecoin.
26th of September 2014	—Tina Hui interviewed Jackson Palmer.
2nd of October 2014	—Fourth reduction in the block reward.
4th of October 2014	—Brad Edwards interviewed lead developer Max Keller.
12th of October 2014	—Tina Hui interviewed Jackson Palmer again.
18th of October 2014	—Josh Wise finished 28th at Talledega in Alabama, USA.
21st of October 2014	—Twitch.tv announced the addition of Dogecoin.
5th of November 2014	—A total of $445,000 raised for the DogeTipBot.
11th of November 2014	—Dogeversary event was announced.
6th of December 2014	—An exchange called Cryptopia added Dogecoin.
6th of December 2014	—Dogeversary event took place in San Francisco.
8th of December 2014	—Last block of the first year at 03:54:38 UTC
8th of December 2014	—First block of the second year at 03:58:09 UTC.

INITIAL DOGECOIN HISTORY

Dogecoin originated from the "Doge" meme pronounced "dohj". Based on a Shiba Inu dog, it won "Meme of the Year 2013". Phrases such as "Such Doge", "Much Happy" and "Wow" in comic sans font are used besides the "Doge".

Jackson Palmer, a marketing professional at Adobe, tweeted the following on his official account (@ummjackson) on the 28th of November 2013 at 00:43 UTC:

"Investing in Dogecoin, pretty sure it's the next big thing. http://tmblr.co/ZXKfHx-duU4J"

At this time, the fiat value of Bitcoin and other cryptocurrencies were reaching all time high market capitalisations. It was also the time at which new coins were being launched every week. Jackson Palmer was following coins such as Bitcoin, Litecoin and Feathercoin. Some people then encouraged Jack to create Dogecoin.

Six days later, Jack bought the domain name www.dogecoin.com on which he placed a picture of a makeshift Dogecoin logo alongside a funny slogan. It was not long before the visitor count of this site increased substantially via retweets.

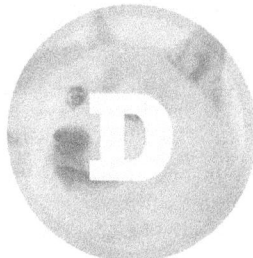

On the 6th of December, a programmer from Oregon, USA called Billy Markus contacted Jack Palmer after seeing the website via direct link on an IRC chatroom. He created the source code and wallet client of Dogecoin ready for launch.

PROOF OF WORK MINING

Proof of work mining is a competitive computerised process which helps to maintain and secure the blockchain in such a way as to verify transactions and prevent double spending. It has been used in Dogecoin since the launch of the coin.

In the general sense of cryptocurrency, those who participate in the activity of mining are called miners. They are general members of the cryptocurrency community who dedicate processing power (hash) of their computers towards solving highly complex mathematical problems and verifying transactions. This process upholds the integrity and security of the network. As such, miners are described as protectors of the network. Each transaction (held within a certain block) is validated before adding it to the blockchain. By doing this, they are rewarded (as an incentive) with newly generated mined coins or transaction fees. These coins are issued by the software in a transparent and predictable way outside of the control of its founders and developers. A miner can be based anywhere in the world as long as they have an internet connection, sufficient knowledge of how one mines and the hardware/software required to do so.

Miners use GPUs (Graphical Processing Units) or CPUs (Central Processing Units) to process transactions by hashing. Also, Application Specific Integrated Circuits (ASICs) allow miners to use customised hardware for faster and lower power mining.

On the 11th of September, the way in which DOGE units of account are verified and added to the blockchain changed at block number 371,337. Instead of being purely PoW, the timestamping method changed to auxiliary proof of work. Miners of Litecoin now helped to secure the Dogecoin network protocol through merge mining. As a consequence, the overall processing power of the network increased.

DOGECOIN BLOCKCHAIN

Every cryptocurrency has a corresponding blockchain within its decentralised network protocol. Dogecoin is no different in this sense. A blockchain is simply described as a general public ledger of all transactions and blocks ever executed since the very first block. In addition, it continuously updates in real time each time a new block is successfully mined. Blocks enter the blockchain in such a manner that each block contains the hash of the previous one. It is therefore utterly resistant to modification along the chain since each block is related to the prior one. Consequently, the problem of doubling-spending is solved.

As a means for the general public to view the blockchain, web developers have created block explorers.

Since the inception of the first block explorer, other websites have been created. Currently available explorers include the following:

- https://dogechain.info/;
- https://bitinfocharts.com/dogecoin/explorer/;
- https://coinplorer.com/DOGE;
- https://prohashing.com/explorer/Dogecoin/;
- https://live.blockcypher.com/doge/;

By visiting and browsing these explorer sites, only the first one is specifically for Dogecoin. It is the official block explorer of Dogecoin on which users can search for a particular block, view network statistics and open a secure online wallet. It was created by Bitcointalk user "GlennMR" on the 9th of December 2013.

DOGECOIN BLOCKCHAIN

Block explorers tend to present different layouts, statistics and charts. Some are more extensive in terms of the information given. Some statistics include:

- **Height of block** —the block number of the network.

- **Time of block** —the time at which the block was timestamped to the blockchain.

- **Transactions** —the number of transactions in that particular block.

- **Total Sent** —the total amount of cryptocurrency sent in that particular block.

- **Block Reward** —how many coins were generated in the block (added to overall coin circulation).

Below is a screenshot of block number one from the block explorer at https://dogechain.info:

Hash	82bc68038f6034c0596b6e313729793a887fded6e92a31fbdf70863f89d9bea2
Previous Block	1a91e3dace36e2be3bf030a65679fe821aa1d6ef92e7c9902eb318182c355691
Next Block:	ea5380659e02a68c073369e502125c634b2fb0aaf351b9360c673368c4f20c96
Height	1
Version	1
Transaction Merkle Root	5f7e779f7600f54e528686e91d5891f3ae226ee907f461692519e549105f521c
Time	2013-12-07 19:55:27 -0800
Difficulty	0.00024414 (Bits: 1e0ffff0)
Nonce	1417875456
Transactions	1
Value out	68.416.00000000

DOGECOIN BLOCK REWARD TABLE

For each and every block successfully mined, verified and added to the blockchain, a certain number of DOGE unit of account are generated. As can be seen below, the number of generated coins per block reduced at certain block heights. Initially, the block reward was random between 0-1,000,000 DOGE. On the 14th of February, it reduced to generate a random reward between 0-500,000 DOGE.

On the 17th of March, the source code was updated to eliminate the randomness of block rewards. A static 250,000 DOGE block reward kicked in.

During the first year of the Dogecoin blockchain (Dogechain), a total of about 96,597,968,750 DOGE were mined.

Block Number	Block Reward	Date of Initial Block	Expected Coins Produced	Cumulative Coin Total
1-100,000	random	08/12/2013	50,000,000,000	50,000,000,000
100,001-144,999	random	14/02/2014	11,249,750,000	61,249,750,000
145,000-199,999	250,000	17/03/2014	13,750,000,000	74,999,750,000
200,000-299,999	125,000	28/04/2014	12,500,000,000	87,499,750,000
300,000-371,336	62,500	15/07/2014	4,458,562,500	91,958,312,500
371,337-399,999	62,500	11/09/2014	1,791,437,500	93,749,750,000
400,000-499,999	31,250	02/10/2014	3,125,000,000	96,874,750,000
500,000-599,999	15,625	14/12/2014	1,562,500,000	98,437,250,000
600,000-	10,000	25/02/2015		

After an expected 98,437,250,000 DOGE coin supply, about 5.256 billion DOGE are mined each year from block number 600,000. This is approximately a 5.34% inflation for the year which began on the 25th of February 2015.

BLOCK TIME OF DOGECOIN

The block time is the average time taken for the network to successfully generate a certain block either by proof of work or proof of stake. Both the reward and time of all blocks generated dictate how the circulation of coins grows over time.

Since the public launch of the blockchain on the 8th of December 2013, the average block has always been stated as sixty seconds. This remained the case even after the hard fork on the 17th of March 2014 (DigiShield update).

Block Number 1	03:55:27 UTC		Block Number 7	03:55:57 UTC
Block Number 2	03:55:33 UTC		Block Number 8	03:56:07 UTC
Block Number 3	03:55:40 UTC		Block Number 9	03:56:09 UTC
Block Number 4	03:55:43 UTC		Block Number 10	03:56:10 UTC
Block Number 5	03:55:49 UTC		Block Number 11	03:56:12 UTC
Block Number 6	03:55:52 UTC		Block Number 12	03:56:17 UTC

As is evident above, the first twelve blocks were mined quickly in only fifty seconds. This was due to the difficulty of mining being very low during this initial period. From the start, the difficulty re-targeting time had been set at four hours.

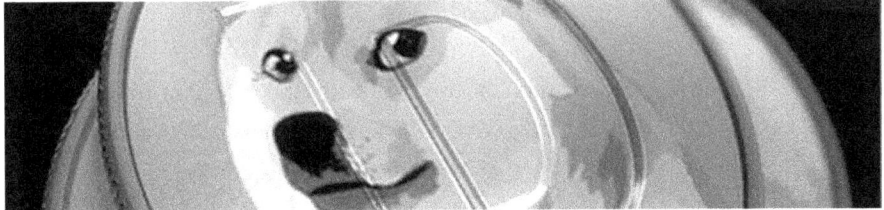

On the 8th of December, block number 491,142 was the last block timestamped to the blockchain during the first year. Taking this into account, each block was generated every 64.21 seconds (on average).

DOGECOIN WALLETS

A wallet is basically a piece of software that can be used on a personal computer, tablet or smartphone. It allows users to store Dogecoins as well as execute transfers of DOGE with other users. Alternatively, it can be described as a means to access the coins from the inseparable blockchain (public transaction ledger). The wallet cryptographically generates and holds the public and private keys necessary to make these transactions possible. The software can be accessed, downloaded and installed from the official page:

• http://dogecoin.com/

Dogecoin wallets have been developed to work on various operating systems such as Windows, Mac and Linux. In addition, users can download the Android or iOS Apple application on their personal smartphone. Users are always notified via forums when an update has been released. Four types of wallet available are:

• **Desktop wallet** —the most secure method to store Dogecoins on one's personal computer.

• **Phone wallet** —users can download and install the Dogecoin wallet application on either their Android or iPhone. This is ideal for sending/receiving DOGE on the go when paying for or selling goods or services.

• **Online wallet** —users can register with and login via their explorer browser. Private keys still remain local and secure on the user's personal computer.

• **Paper wallet** —users can generator a secure paper wallet on which a public and private key (usually with corresponding QR codes) is displayed

WHAT IS PROOF OF WORK/STAKE?

Proof of work and proof of stake are both referred to collectively as timestamping methods. They are the methods used to secure the network protocol of a certain cryptocurrency in order to sustain decentralisation and validate transactions. Therefore, no third party needs to be trusted to verify and then add transactions the blockchain.

Proof of work mining is currently used in the decentralised network protocol of Bitcoin thanks to the research by Satoshi Nakamoto. Miners commit the processing (hashing) power of their computers towards successfully finding blocks either individually or as part of a group with other miners (mining pool). As the cumulative hash of the network increases, the network becomes more secure.

Proof of stake was independently discovered by Sunny King after he studied the work of Nakamoto. It was introduced into Peercoin alongside proof of work on the 19th of August 2012. Users of the wallet client help to secure the network by keeping their clients active. When coins arrive in a given wallet address, they begin to age. After a certain pre-determined time, a user receives coins (a stake) in their personal desktop wallet client.

Proof of stake is widely accepted as the environmentally friendly way to timestamp transactions to the blockchain instead of the high energy cost of proof of work.

Many other coins have implemented proof of stake into their network protocols since its introduction. Novacoin was the first cryptocurrency to adopt proof of stake into their network protocol on the 9th of February 2013.

In 2014, the developers of Reddcoin built an innovative timestamping algorithm of their own called Proof of Stake Velocity.

FIRST YEAR DOGECOIN EXCHANGES

Unlike many other cryptocurrencies, Dogecoin was very successful in terms of the number of exchanges it began to trade on. In the space of just three weeks since block number one, a total of six known exchanges had already added Dogecoin to their trading platform. Cryptsy, Coins-e, Vircurex and Bter still trade Dogecoin at the time of publication of this book. From the 8th of December 2013 to the 30th of November 2015, a total of sixteen known exchanges (added in the first year) have closed down due to server problems, hackings or other dubious activities.

Dates on which Dogecoin was added to the below exchanges have been discovered by reading announcements on official forum threads or by visiting the relevant cryptocurrency exchange in question. Throughout the first year, thirty two known cryptocurrency exchanges added Dogecoin to their trading platform. These were:

Name of Exchange	Trading Against	Status	Date Added
Coined Up	BTC and LTC	CLOSED	12th of December 2013
Cryptsy	BTC, LTC and XRP	ACTIVE	18th of December 2013
Coins-e	BTC and LTC	ACTIVE	19th of December 2013
Vircurex	BTC	ACTIVE	20th of December 2013
Bter	BTC and CNY	ACTIVE	23rd of December 2013
CoinEx	BTC and LTC	CLOSED	25th of December 2013
BTC-8	BTC and CNY	CLOSED	1st of January 2014
AltQuick.co	USD	ACTIVE	8th of January 2014
OpenEx	BTC	CLOSED	8th of January 2014
C-Cex	BTC and USD	ACTIVE	18th of January 2014
Cryptokopen.eu	EUR	CLOSED	18th of January 2014

FIRST YEAR DOGECOIN EXCHANGES

Name of Exchange	Trading Against	Status	Date Added
Poloniex	BTC	ACTIVE	22nd of January 2014
Cryptorush.in	BTC and LTC	CLOSED	24th of January 2014
Vault of Satoshi	USD and CAD	CLOSED	29th of January 2014
Swisscex	BTC	CLOSED	1st of February 2014
BTC38	BTC and CNY	ACTIVE	11th of February 2014
Newaltex	BTC	CLOSED	11th of February 2014
Bittrex	BTC	ACTIVE	13th of February 2014
MintPal	BTC	CLOSED	19th of February 2014
Kraken	BTC	ACTIVE	20th of February 2014
Comkort	BTC and LTC	CLOSED	20th of February 2014
useCryptos	BTC	ACTIVE	22nd of February 2014
Coin Market	BTC and USD	CLOSED	14th of March 2014
AGX.io	BTC	CLOSED	15th of March 2014
BTC100	BTC and CNY	ACTIVE	19th of April 2014
CoinNext	BTC	CLOSED	13th of May 2014
HitBTC	BTC, LTC, USD and EUR	ACTIVE	3rd of June 2014
Kingcoiny	BTC	CLOSED	4th of June 2014
mcxNOW	BTC	CLOSED	8th of June 2014
CEX.IO	BTC and LTC	ACTIVE	20th of August 2014
Cryptonit	BTC	ACTIVE	18th of September 2014
Cryptopia	BTC and LTC	ACTIVE	6th of December 2014

CURRENT DOGECOIN EXCHANGES

A cryptocurrency exchange is a site on which registered users can buy or sell Dogecoin against BTC, LTC, USD and so on. Some exchanges require users to fully register by submitting certain documentation including proof of identity and address. On the other hand, most exchanges only require users to register with a simple username and password with the use of a currently held e-mail account.

As of the 18th of October 2015, the following cryptocurrency exchanges were actively trading Dogecoin. This was by no means an exhaustive list:

Exchange	Location	Exchange	Location
AllCoin	British Virgin Islands	Cryptsy	United States
Bitcoin Indonesia	Indonesia	HitBTC	China
Bitorado		Jubi	China
Bittrex	United States	Justcoin	Norway
Bittylicious	England	Kraken	
BTC100	China	LiteBit.eu	The Netherlands
BTC38	China	Livecoin	
Bleutrade	Brazil	NIX-E	Russia
Bter	China	Poloniex	United States
BX Thailand	Thailand	SouthXchange	
C-Cex		The Rock Trading	
CCEDK	Denmark	Use Cryptos	Brazil
CEX.IO		Vircurex	China
Coinsquare		Yuanbaohui	
Cryptopia		YoBit	

DOGECOIN COMMUNITY

A community is a social unit or network that shares common values and goals. It derives from the Old French word "comuntee". This, in turn, originates from "communitas" in Latin (communis; things held in common). Dogecoin has a community consisting of an innumerable number of individuals who have the coin's well being and future goal at heart. These individuals almost always prefer fictitious names with optional corresponding "avatars". Notable members of the community are Jackson Palmer, Max Keller, Josh Mohland, Ben Dournberg, Billy Markus and David Dvorak.

At the time of publication, there are official social media sites on which discussion and development of Dogecoin take place. These are:

- **Bitcointalk**   -https://bitcointalk.org/index.php?topic=361813.0
- **Facebook**   -https://www.facebook.com/OfficialDogecoin?fref=ts
- **Official Forum**   -http://doges.org/
- **Reddit**   -https://www.reddit.com/r/dogecoin
- **Twitter**   -https://twitter.com/dogecoin

In addition to these, there is a Dogecoin news site on which independent journalists publish articles about the coin:

- **News Site**   -http://www.dailydoge.org/

In essence, the community surrounding and participating in the development of Dogecoin is the backbone of the coin. Without a following, the prospects of future adoption and utilisation are starkly limited. Dogecoin belongs to all those who use it, not just to the founder who initially created it.

FIRST YEAR HISTORY OF DOGECOIN

LIST OF CHAPTERS

THE BIRTH OF DOGECOIN ON BITCOINTALK

DECEMBER 2013

I.   Bitcointalk forum thread created for Dogecoin.

II.   Dogecoin network protocol launched publicly.

III.   Coined Up was the first cryptocurrency exchange to trade Dogecoin.

IV.   Dogecoin began to trade on a further five cryptocurrency exchanges.

V.   Dogecoin version 1.3 wallet client released.

On the 8th of December 2013 at 03:55:25 UTC, a Bitcointalk user fictitiously named "Dogecoin" announced a new cryptocurrency called Dogecoin, DOGE. This official Dogecoin Bitcointalk thread was given the title "[ANN][DOGE] Dogecoin - very currency - many coin - wow". Two seconds later, the first block was added to the blockchain (68,416 DOGE were generated at this block). The very first response on this thread was made by user "eon89" at 04:03:14 UTC on the same day:

> "Someone get a pool going now."

Less than one minute later (36 seconds), user "MrDjAK" was the second user to post a comment on the thread:

> "all shares rejected why?"

> **Block #1 (Reward 68,416) December 8th 2013 at 03:55:27 AM UTC**

As is evident from the block distribution table show on page 24, the number of DOGE rewarded to miners who successfully solved blocks was random. Between blocks 1 and 100,000, the reward had been pre-determined to generate a random number between 0 and 1,000,000 DOGE (average 500,000 DOGE over the period). Taking into account the block time of one minute, it was expected that the average reward would halve in about 69 days (15th of February 2014). By that time, a total of roughly 50 billion DOGE (half the supply) will have been mined.

Also on the 8th of December, the official Dogecoin Subreddit was created at 12:36:11 UTC as well as a forum at www.doges.org by user "Drexme".

On the 9th of December, user "GlennMR" created the first Dogecoin block explorer at http://dogechain.info/chain/Dogecoin. On the same day, the first independent article was published by Danny Vega. It was titled "Dogecoin: 5 Fast Facts You Need to Know":

1. One Dogecoin (Doge) Is Worth Approximately 1/100 Cent.
2. Wow, A Total of 100 Billion Doge Can Be Mined
3. Dogecoin's Wallet Appears to Be Based on Luckycoin
4. There Are Over 500 People Actively Mining and Creating Doge
5. Such Dogecoiners Appear to Be Very Bullish About The Future Value of Dogecoin

http://heavy.com/tech/2013/12/dogecoin-what-is-shibe-cryptocurrenc/

In reference to the first point above, members of the community were trading Dogecoin before trading on any exchanges existed. A trade between two Reddit users called "ottothepup" (the seller) and "Ultra1996" (the buyer) occurred. A total of 10,000 DOGE were bought by "Ultra1996" for $1. This was one of hundreds (possibly thousands) of trades between users on Reddit and elsewhere, but it was evidence that a price conversion rate existed early on.

On the 10th of December at 01:46:59 UTC, user "shigoga" proposed three new variations of a Dogecoin logo design:

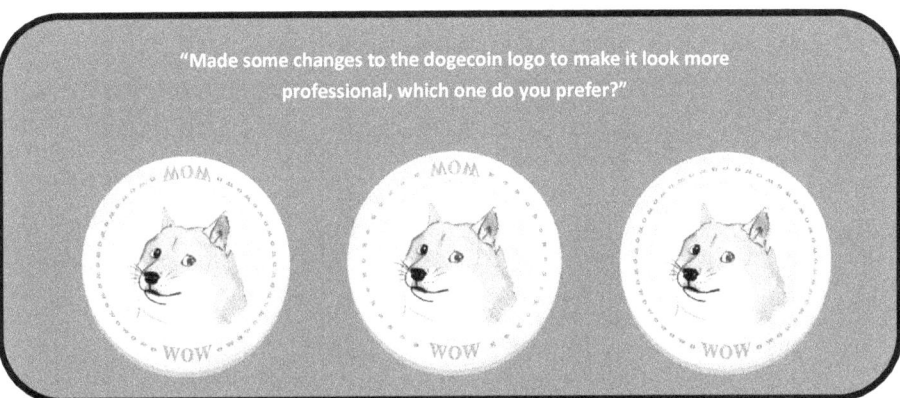

On the following day at 09:36:29 UTC , user "Dogecoin" made an announcement regarding the current coin logo (original logo can be seen on page 34):

User "viatorek" commented on the above two new coin logo designs by saying:

On the 12th of December, the first cryptocurrency exchange called Coined Up added Dogecoin to their trading platform. Both the DOGE/BTC and DOGE/LTC markets were established. An announcement was made at 05:41:06 UTC by user "pete_coinedup" on the official Dogecoin Bitcointalk thread:

> "Hello,
>
> CoinedUp.com - the FREE crypto exchange, now has a DOGE/BTC market as well as a DOGE mining pool.
>
> https://CoinedUp.com
>
> mining pool: [stratum] [0% fee] [prop payout]
> [fast & reliable - Virginia, USA servers] [Donations such Appreciated]
>
> http://miner.coindup.com/doge
>
> ...many enjoy!"

On the same day, v1.1 of the wallet client was released. At 07:40:20 UTC, user "Dogecoin" made the following post on the official Dogecoin Bitcointalk thread:

> "Version 1.1 of the client has been released.
> Generally minor cosmetic changes, but it should sync better."

According to the website www.cryptocoincharts.info, the Bitcoin Satoshi value of one unit of DOGE account was highly volatile on Coined Up. In addition, the daily trading volume on that exchange grew considerably over four days:

	Price	Low	Open	Close	High	Volume (BTC)
12th Dec	9.5	1	10	9	25	2.08044
13th Dec	10.5	4	9	12	-	25.9893
14th Dec	41	18	48	34	-	122.679
15th Dec	31.5	9	13	50	-	472.32

On the 15th of December, user "Luror" at 14:46:01 UTC made the following comment on the official Dogecoin Bitcointalk thread:

"DogeCoin is #18 on coinmarketcap.com"

This was the day on which the coin was added to the above website. Its initial coin market capitalisation on this website was approximately $3.5 million.

Two days later, an article was published on the website http://spelunk.in titled "The Humans behind Dogecoin". Written by Pinguino, it mentioned that the coin had taken the Internet by storm one week previously. In the article, the value of one Dogecoin was quoted as being about $0.00025 on that day. They also interviewed the co-creators of Dogecoin called Jack Palmer and Billy Markus. This transcript is in the appendix of this book on pages 123 to 129.

http://spelunk.in/2013/12/17/discover-dogecoin-currency-for-the-internet/

On the 18th of December, user "BitJohn" at 22:12:51 UTC notified the community on the official Dogecoin Bitcointalk thread that Dogecoin had been initiated for active trading on Cryptsy. He was quoted as saying:

"Welcome Dogecoin DOGE miners and traders and welcome to the Cryptsy.com family of coins."

This exchange launched on the 20th of May 2013. It is based in Delray Beach, Florida, USA. It has become one of the most reputable cryptocurrency trading exchanges currently active today. Before it was possible to trade on Cryptsy, the following were popular ways to buy/sell/trade with Dogecoin:

http://doges.org/index.php?board=3.0
http://www.reddit.com/r/dogemarket
http://coinedup.com/OrderBook?market=DOGE&base=BTC

Shibes (users of Dogecoin) were very happy that Dogecoin had got onto the Cryptsy exchange platform. Initially, the time it took to deposit Dogecoins into the exchange was longer than people expected.

On the 19th of December, user "Dogecoin" at 14:52:13 UTC notified the community of an updated wallet client. It had been released the day before on github. He said:

> "Version 1.2 has been released. As more people adopt this release, the syncing issues should subside.
>
> The issue was, with the incredible amount of demand and clients out there, everyone was getting filtered into 1 IRC channel, causing massive flooding and disconnects. An awesome member of a community added a Seed DNS server for us for supernodes, as well as increased the number of IRC channels so people can actually connect to each other.
>
> (Only windows client available at the moment, Mac will be released shortly)"

This update was not mandatory. It was released in order fix the synchronisation problems faced by some users (problems downloading the blockchain).

On the same day, the value of one DOGE unit of account had increased over 300 percent during the three preceding days. In fiat dollar terms, one DOGE went from ~$0.00026 to ~$0.00095. However, its value crashed 80% three days later.

Also on the 19th of December, Coins-e became the third cryptocurrency exchange to implement the trading pair DOGE/BTC on their platform:

> www.coins-e.com/exchange/DOGE_BTC

Coins-e went live in late June 2013. It was possible to trade about fifteen different cryptocurrencies from the beginning. Over 50,000 people have signed up to the exchange since it launched.

It is still active today, but only very small trade volumes exist on it.

https://www.youtube.com/watch?v=H3oiThw2RxE

Besides its addition to three cryptocurrency exchanges, Dogecoin had begun to inspire. An example of this was the video uploaded to YouTube by "Wunkolo" on the 19th of December. This video titled "dogecoin.avi" had about 259,000 views up until the 27th of October 2015.

In addition to the video, many articles were written about Dogecoin by independent journalists. Two of these were:

"What is Dogecoin? The Meme that Became the Hot New Virtual Currency"
By David Gilbert

"Bitcoin Alternative Dogecoin Soars 900% As Other Crypto-Currencies Suffer"
By Alistair Charlton

Both articles were published on the International Business Times website on the 20th December

On the 20th of December, the third exchange in as many days added Dogecoin. On the www.doges.org forum at 02:50:03 UTC, user "PSFL" made the following post:

"https://vircurex.com/welcome/index?alt=doge&base=btc&locale=en

Hopefully there will be some decent volume there."

On the 23rd of December, cryptocurrencies were discussed on the television channel Bloomberg. A video of the discussion titled "Bitcoin Isn't Alone: Newer Currencies Popping Up" was published in which Matt Miller talked about the multitude of Bitcoin alternatives in the crypto space. Dogecoin (pronounced Dog-e-coin by Matt Miller) was mentioned. The footage was part of the program called "In The Loop" and the segment of this program was the "12 Days of Bitcoin".

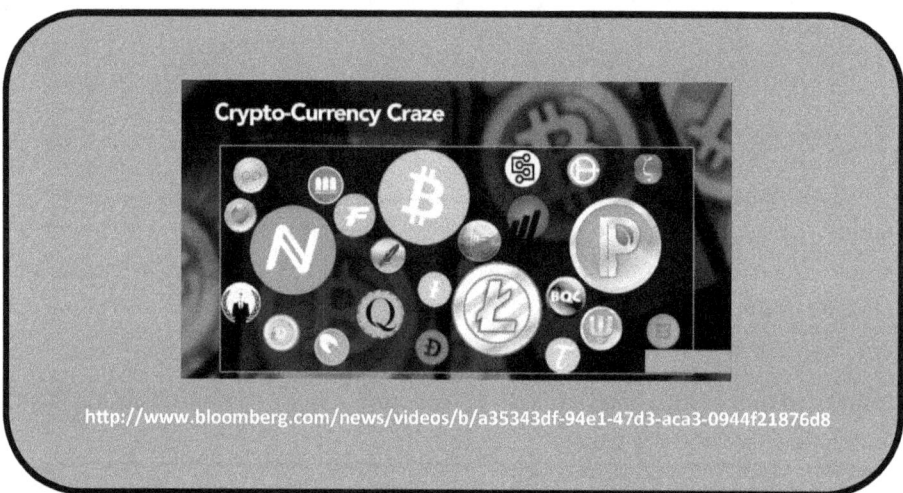

Besides the above media attention, the first Chinese exchange called Bter incorporated Dogecoin into its trading platform on the 23rd of December.

On the 25th of December at 12:33:51 UTC, user "captainfuture" said:

"DOGE added to our pools and exchange:

https://coinex.pw/trade/doge_btc

https://coinex.pw/mining/pools/DOGE"

On their official Twitter page, their slogan was "the only realtime cryptocurrency exchange with integrated mining". This exchange no longer exists.

One day later, the trading pair DOGE/LTC was added to CoinEx.

Also on Christmas Day, the first major theft of Dogecoin happened from an online wallet called Dogewallet. Millions of Dogecoin were stolen by means of the hacker or group of hackers accessing the system. Nevertheless, it had the effect of promoting the coin via Twitter on which people discussed the theft.

In order to help people who had had coins stolen, the community initiated an online campaign called "SaveDogemas". Donations were sent to the following wallet address (private key stored securely by Brian Worley):

DCCpdXmwD9TjqnXvmm7NrrBQt2nBKEPDSt

On the 26th of December at 07:33:10 UTC , user "Dogecoin" said:

"The 1.3 update is mandatory, please make sure you update. Windows release can be downloaded at:
https://github.com/dogecoin/dogecoin/releases/download/v1.3/dogecoin-qt-v13-Win.zip

To address dust issues / microtransaction attacks, a minimum transaction size of Ð1 has been introduced to prevent spamming and dust gathering on the blockchain, and a transaction fee of Ð2 applied for transactions under this amount. A Ð1 transaction fee will apply for all other transactions.

Issues may be experienced if you do not update.
Pool owners, please update to the latest dogecoind ASAP.

If anyone can compile to OS X and share here, it would be greatly appreciated. Github repo @ https://github.com/dogecoin/dogecoin

Thanks all!"

On the 27th of December at 05:11:31 UTC, user "Dogecoin" said:

"1.3 binary for OS X now available @ https://github.com/dogecoin/dogecoin/releases/download/v1.3/dogecoin-qt-v13-Mac.zip and fromhttp://dogecoin.com

Thanks to http://www.reddit.com/user/psylence519 for help with OS X building."

On the 28th of December, the Dogecoin Subreddit was the subreddit of the day. Two shibes were asked three questions relating to Dogecoin:

How did you find out about dogecoin?

ottothepup: "I found out about dogecoin when browsing /r/supershibe and somebody linked it."

42points : "From Bitcointalk forums. I saw a new coin and thought I'd give it a go. First time mining."

How many dogecoin do you have?

ottothepup: "I have around 2.5 million DOGE

42points: "Just under 200,000 left. I mined just under 3.9 million and have stopped mining. Lost 1.2 million (stolen). Donated about 2.5mil to beggars, faucets and people who have helped me to promote dogecoin."

Do you think cryptocurrencies are the future?

Ottothepup: "I do not think they're entirely the future for the whole world, but I do believe they're the future for the internet and their trades."

42points: "Yes. Just like how torrents changed the way people get music content bitcoin will change the way people pay for things (especially online). It's unstoppable. The world is going to have to get used to it. I expect far more resistance than what the music companies gave us before they decided to jump onboard with itunes, etc."

On the last day of the year, user "scarface" posted the following at 20:16:48 UTC:

"official dogecoin mobile wallet released

https://play.google.com/store/apps/details?id=de.langerhans.wallet

now you can pay for products with dogecoin on the go with your android device

based on the bitcoin mobile wallet"

Other events which occurred in the month of December were:

- The first Dogecoin mining pool at http://doge.scryptpools.com/ was announced by user "Phonetic" at 09:47:43 UTC on the 8th of December.

- On the 14th of December, some people were so keen to get hold of the coin via eBay. An auction for one million DOGE ended at 16:11:42 PST on this day. The winning bid was $810 (31 bids, 8 bidders, one day duration).

- On the 14th of December, the market capitalisation (value of all coins mined) surpassed $1 million for the first time.

- On the 15th of December, the first version of Dogetipbot went live on Reddit thanks to Josh Mohland and David Dvorak.

- On the 19th of December, the market capitalisation (the value of all Dogecoin ever mined) surpassed $10 million for the first time.

- Number of Dogecoin mined surpassed 10 billion on the 20th of December.

- On Xmas Day, the number of subscribers on the Dogecoin Subreddit (16,062) surpassed the number subscribed to the Litecoin Subreddit (15,674).

- The official Dogecoin Facebook group was created on the 29th of December. It had a total of about 2,000 likes in the first 24 hours.

Shibe "intisun" posted a link to the image below on the Dogecoin subreddit on the 29th of December at 07:10:11 UTC (http://i.imgur.com/4XYGfKz.jpg)

OVER $30,000 RAISED FOR THE
JAMAICAN BOBSLEIGH TEAM

JANUARY 2014

I.   Dogecoin version 1.4 wallet client released.

II.   AltQuick.co was the first to introduce direct purchase of DOGE with USD.

III.   Target to raise $30,000 for the Jamaican Bobsleigh Team achieved.

IV.   Market capitalisation of Dogecoin surpassed $50 million.

V.   Dogecoin version 1.5 wallet client released.

In the early hours of New Years Day, the second Chinese cryptocurrency exchange added the trading pair DOGE/CNY. This was announced on Reddit by user "otakupcgamer" at 02:06:51 UTC on the same day:

> "DOGE is on btc-8.com another chinese exchange with DOGE/CNY Pair.
>
> http://btc-8.com/?DOGE_CNY"

BTC-8 no longer actively trades cryptocurrency.

According to www.bitinfocharts.com, the average price of one unit of DOGE account was ~$0.00042 on the first day of 2014. Corresponding Bitcoin Satoshi values of one DOGE unit of account on Coined Up, Cryptsy and Coins-e were 57, 56 and 57 respectively. One Bitcoin Satoshi equals 0.00000001 BTC.

On the 5th of January at 09:52:27 UTC, a mandatory wallet client was released. Wallet holders, cryptocurrency exchanges and mining pools were urged to update as soon as possible. User "Dogecoin" was quoted as saying:

> "DogeCoin has been updated to v1.4, adding checkpoints for the correct fork. Please update your clients and daemons immediately. See http://www.reddit.com/r/dogecoin/comments/1ug958/psa_dogecoin_wallet_version_14_released_you_must/
>
> If you are having issues syncing / your blockchain is messed up, follow the instructions from http://www.reddit.com/r/dogecoin/comments/1ug9h1/syncing_from_13_will_very_likely_put_you_on_the/ to get you back to the correct chain."

On the 8th of January, a bounty of 1,500,000 DOGE was pledged by Reddit user "Tuxedage" to encourage tech savvy individuals to develop the first Electrum Wallet for Dogecoin (one already existed for Bitcoin). This wallet would allow the end user to access the whole blockchain online without the need to download it onto their personal computer. All other data including wallet files (wallet.dat) would still remain local and secure on the wallet holder's personal computer. At this point in time, the blockchain had reached a size of about 1.4 gigabytes. A significant proportion of people were struggling to download and store it offline.

Also on this day, the first exchange platform to allow direct DOGE to USD trading went live. AltQuick.co launched this method of trade, besides others including Litecoin, Namecoin, Feathercoin and Peercoin, with USD . However, there was a difference in the manner of buying and selling on this exchange. Leon Pick from Finance Magnate described it as follows:

> "Parties interested in buying DOGE first place their order online. If the order is matched by a seller, they then need to physically visit a U.S. branch of either Bank of America, Wells Fargo, US Bank or JP Morgan Chase to make a cash deposit. Once confirmed, the coins are credited to the account. Sellers deposit their cryptcoins into a specially designated escrow address, and then "receive cash deposits from buyers on AltQuick.co instantly", although it remains to be clarified exactly how."

On the 11th of January, the trading pair DOGE/BTC was reported as being the highest of all the other 130 pairs in terms of daily trading volume on Cryptsy:

First: DOGE/BTC; Second: WDC/BTC; Third: LTC/BTC; Fourth: QRK/BTC; Fifth: DOGE/LTC.

Four days later, the market capitalisation (the total USD value of all coins generated) of Dogecoin surpassed $10 million for the first time since the 19th of December 2013. In the early hours (UTC) of the 15th of January, the community were made aware of the following figures:

#13 on www.coinmarketcap.com (including pre-mined cryptocurrencies)

Market Capitalisation: ~$10,146,114
Daily trading volume (last 24 hours): ~$660,245
Dogecoin mined: ~28,180,597,034 DOGE
24 hour % change in market capitalisation: +33.18%

On the 18th of January, Dogecoin surpassed Primecoin in terms of market capitalisation. On the same day, it also went above Worldcoin, Megacoin and Quark to become the fifth highest cryptocurrency on the market (excluding pre-mined coins such as Ripple, Mastercoin and Nxt).

Also on the 18th of January at 14:49:15 UTC, user "bittick" made an announcement about another exchange addition:

"Hi guys,

We have added DOGE to http://cryptokopen.eu which allows regular users to buy doge directly.

Please donate for us to be able to keep DOGE on the website a bit longer!

DRZjjsHGKt2piMYytRAN7ZujdfiZ5Bavjy

Thank you!"

Later on the same day, the first mention on Bitcointalk of the campaign to help the Jamaican Bobsleigh Team was posted by user "itsybitsy" at 16:00:05 UTC:

> "Guys please donate to the official Dogecoin Foundation fund to finance the Jamaican Olympic Bobsled Team so they can go to Sotchi:
> http://dogesled.dogecointousd.com/
>
> If you use Twitter then tell the team @JamaicaOlympics about your donation including the hashtags #dogecoin and #dogesled
>
> To the Olympics then to the moon!"

A few hours later at 21:43:21 UTC, user "fcrypto7" posted:

> **"FELLOW SHIBES! WE GOING TO OLYMPIC GAMES! IT'S FANTASTIC OPPORTUNITY! PLS DONATE!**
>
> **2014 Winter Olympic Jamaican Bobsled Team!**
>
> For the first time since 2002, the Jamaican bobsled team is expected to qualify for the winter Olympics. They are currently trying to raise donations to get them there, so before we reach the moon we want to make a pit stop at Sochi.
>
> This is our chance to prove to the world the power of dogecoin and do something truly great for a national team with a inspirational legacy. Feel the rhythm, feel the ride, get on down, it's bobsled time! How to donate?
>
> Visit: http://foundation.dogecoin.com/roadmap
> Click "Charities"
> Send some doges to address from "2014 Winter Olympic Jamaican Bobsled Team!""

At a certain time on the 18th of January, Jack Palmer uploaded the first introductory Dogecoin promotional video to YouTube titled "Dogecoin - such currency". It can be found at the following URL address:

> https://www.youtube.com/watch?v=7SkMT3WqzLM&feature=youtu.be

On the 19th of January at 00:56:20 UTC, user "Dogecoin" said:

> "Dogecoin v1.4.1 released for windows. This fixes the crash bug when encrypting a wallet or doing 'getmininginfo' on certain windows platforms.
>
> https://github.com/dogecoin/dogecoin/releases/tag/v1.4.1"

Version 1.4.1 was actually recorded as being released one day previously.

One day had passed since fundraising for the Jamaican Bobsleigh Team consisting of Winston Watts and Marvin Dixon began. They had already qualified for the event for the first time since 2002 but required money in order to get them to the Sochi Winter Olympic Games. At a specific time on the 19th of January, a total of 4 million DOGE (~$3,000) in funds had been donated. A tweet was posted by @Dogeboard at 04:26 UTC one day earlier:

> "@JamaicaOlympics The #dogecoin community is prepared to contribute sizable funding for the bobsled team. But we need your help! #dogesled"

On the 20th of January, the fundraising target of $30,000 was hit. A total of roughly 26,000,000 DOGE had been donated. Liam Butler, the head of the Dogecoin Foundation at the time, was quoted as saying:

> "Myself and Jackson Palmer (the creator of Dogecoin) were at a local pub trivia in Sydney when we noticed the value of Dogecoin had more than doubled since we'd last checked so we raced back to my house to ensure we could get the best price for the donations in a form the team could actually use.
> As much as we have faith in Dogecoin to become the community currency of the internet, we still understand that the team need to buy their airfares in a fiat currency."

Liam Butler managed to secure about $25,000 from the DOGE to BTC to USD exchange rate. Donations kept coming in after the goal had been achieved.

User "fcrypto7" submitted a post on the official Dogecoin Bitcointalk thread at 17:28:04 UTC. A list of media sources were:

> "WOW Shibes! News like that we can find in very many places . We did it!
>
> http://www.buzzfeed.com/tomphillips/internet-raises-over-30000-in-dogecoins-to-send
>
> http://www.ibtimes.co.uk/dogecoin-community-wants-get-jamaican-bobsleigh-team-sochi-2014-1432989
>
> http://news.cnet.com/8301-1023_3-57617477-93/dogecoin-raises-$30000-for-jamaican-bobsleigh-team/
>
> http://uk.news.yahoo.com/dogecoin-community-wants-jamaican-bobsleigh-team-sochi-2014-094403535.html#almITNo
>
> http://www.theverge.com/2014/1/20/5326932/jamaican-bobsled-olympic-crowdfunding-campaigns-raising-money
>
> and many more"

In the early hours (UTC) of the 21st of January, the market capitalisation had surged to a peak of roughly $76 million. Dogecoin also surpassed Bitcoin in terms of daily trading volume (~$21.7 million). According to www.cryptocoincharts.info, the Bitcoin Satoshi values of one unit of DOGE account on this day were:

	Price	Low	Open	Close	High	Volume (BTC)
Coined Up	185	142	143	227	260	341.77
Cryptsy	227	202	231	241	298	124.807
Coins-e	190	142	144	236	258	110.174
Vircurex	189.5	143	144	235	268	1002.56
Bter	193	143	145	241	298	3261.89

On the next day, active trading of Dogecoin against Bitcoin began on Poloniex. This was about three days after the exchange was established on the 19th of January.

On the 28th of January at 03:27:41 UTC, user "Dogecoin" said:

> "DogeCoin has been updated to v1.5, rebasing the code on the most recent version of Litecoin, adding much security. Heavily recommended to upgrade.
> Seehttp://www.reddit.com/r/dogecoin/comments/1wc77t/
> psa_v15_of_dogecoin_officially_released_make_sure/for more info."

Four further exchanges had incorporated Dogecoin during January. These were:

Exchange	Date Added	Status
OpenEx	8th of January	Closed down on the 27th of March 2014
C-Cex	18th of January	Added on this date, but trading began in late January
Cryptorush	24th of January	No longer exists due to security issues (hacking)
Vault of Satoshi	29th of January	Active trading began one day later

Other events which occurred in the month of January were:

- On the 12th of January, the Dogecoin Foundation, the non-profit entity created by Dogecoin's founders, was established. As an organisation, it accepts donations which are used to fund a variety of charities, promotional events and development projects.

- On the 19th of January, the first ever Dogecoin meet-up was announced. It would take place in New York City from 6:30 PM to 9:00 PM on the 7th of February. The event organizer was Ben Doernberg.

- Jack Palmer released version 1.5 of the wallet client on the 28th of January. It changed the code base to Litecoin 0.8.6.2.

- On the 30th of January, 50,000 DOGE were donated to provide pizza for the homeless thanks to "/u/myniga562". Following on from this, another 2 million DOGE were raised for homeless people. On the same day, 4 million DOGE were raised to send another athlete (Indian) to the Olympic games.

ALL TIME HIGH MARKET CAPITALISATION
OF 2014 REACHED
FEBRUARY 2014

I.   Palmer announced Dogecoin will not be capped at 100 billion total coins.

II.   Fund raising target of 20 million DOGE achieved for Doge4Kids.

III.   First Dogecoin meet-up took place in New York City.

IV.   First reduction of the block reward at block number 100,001.

V.   Dogecoin began active trading on eight cryptocurrency exchanges.

Over the past seven to eight weeks, Dogecoin had become one of the most popular, most tipped and most traded cryptocurrencies alongside Bitcoin, Litecoin and Peercoin. It had already got noticed by many reputable media sources as a result of helping the Jamaican Bobsleigh Team. It was hard, or even impossible, to find any other cryptocurrency which had achieved the same feat.

On the 2nd of February, the developers of Dogecoin announced that the total number of coins planned for mining won't be capped at 100 billion DOGE. Reddit user "imbiat" posted the following at 06:27:00 UTC:

> "Dogecoin was meant to be capped at 100 billion coins, but the code does not actually implement this. It will grow beyond 100 billion coins because the block reward stays at 10,000 indefinitely.
> The developers have decided to leave the code as is."

Some members of the community were disappointed, fearful or very upset at hearing this news. By not having a cap on the total number of coins to be mined, they were worried about how this would effect the long term value of the coin. Besides, Bitcoin and Litecoin have a hard limit on how many coins can ever be mined. On the 2nd of February, "SunliMin" at 23:49:47 UTC on Reddit posted:

"We have a 5 billion coin inflation rate, and that happens to be 5% for the first year once we hit 100 billion. After a year, that 5% will not be 5%. It will be 5/105=4.7%. In the year 2019 we will be at 4%. The reason is because our 5 billion is a constant. It is NOT a compounding 5% like most fiat currencys have. This is NOT the same as compound interest where it will sky rocket out of control. This is a set amount. A constant. Remember that."

Following on from the Jamaican fundraising campaign, another worthwhile cause was initiated. On the 2nd of February, the Doge4Kids campaign began:

"Over the past few weeks, we as a community have done some amazing things. Today, we'd like to announce our latest initiative - Doge 4 Kids.

The Dogecoin Foundation is partnering with the amazing folks at charity 4 Paws for Ability and crowdfunding platform Crowdtilt to help provide service dogs to children in need.

As part of this campaign, we're hoping to raise 20 million DOGE, the equivalent of US$30,000 by the end of February, 2014. You contributions are appreciated, and we hope to go above and beyond our target in helping this cause.

Learn more and donate at: http://doge4kids.org/

To the mooon!
Help The Dogecoin Foundation and 4 Paws for Ability raise US$30,000 to pair trained service dogs with children in need."

On the 4th of February, 7.9 million DOGE had been raised for the charity "4 Paws for Ability". At this rate, the target amount would be easily achieved.

On the 6th of February at 16:31:09 UTC, a user called "VeryFluffyUnicorn" posted the following on the Dogecoin Subreddit:

"In 6 days In 3(!!!) days the dogecoin community donated 20 Million Ð.
Thank you to everyone who helped achieve this goal!

Edit: We need another 3 million to actually reach 30k USD. Donate here:
http://www.reddit.com/r/dogecoin/comments/1x6vhr/
at_5pm_est_someone_from_4_paws_for_ability/"

One of the www.dailydoge.org independent journalists called Howard praised the community for all the hard work and generosity shown:

"This is a truly heart-warming story that makes me proud to be a part of the Dogecoin community. What was once viewed as a "joke" currency is now changing lives around the world. I would like to thank the CrowdTilt, Doge4Kids, and the Dogecoin foundation for making all of this possible.
Keep up the good work Shibes. Our charitable spirit knows no bounds."

One day after the above success, the very first Dogecoin meet-up happened in New York City at the Bitcoin Centre (rented out by Nick Spanos). Organised by Ben Dournberg, it was an event to celebrate Dogecoin and bring together members of the community. People from the "Occupy Wall Street" crowd were also present at the event.

Thirteen days later, a video titled "Dogeparty 2014" was uploaded to YouTube. It was a short film documentary produced by Adam Cornelius and Chris Higgins:

https://www.youtube.com/watch?v=E-W1weeK2UA&feature=youtu.be

On the 8th of February, user "Laika1954" at 11:44:52 UTC posted the following about the latest update (not mandatory) of the wallet client. It allowed users to look up transactions on the Dogechain from within the wallet client:

"We're happy to announce the release of Dogecoin version 1.5.1!

This release incorporates a range of updates from community contributors, some much needed bug fixes, plus some cool treats brought down-stream from the recent Bitcoin 0.9 release candidate.

Thanks to everyone who helped make this release possible, the entire community appreciates it. We recommend all users update to the latest version and please report any issues you may encounter. As always, backup your wallet.dat file before updating (just to be safe)."

Dogecoin had sustained a market capitalisation above ~$50,000,000 since the 21st of January. On the 9th of February, this measure of the fiat value of all the Dogecoins ever mined began to increase again. The Bitcoin Satoshi value of one unit of DOGE account began to rise (please see the chart from Cryptsy below):

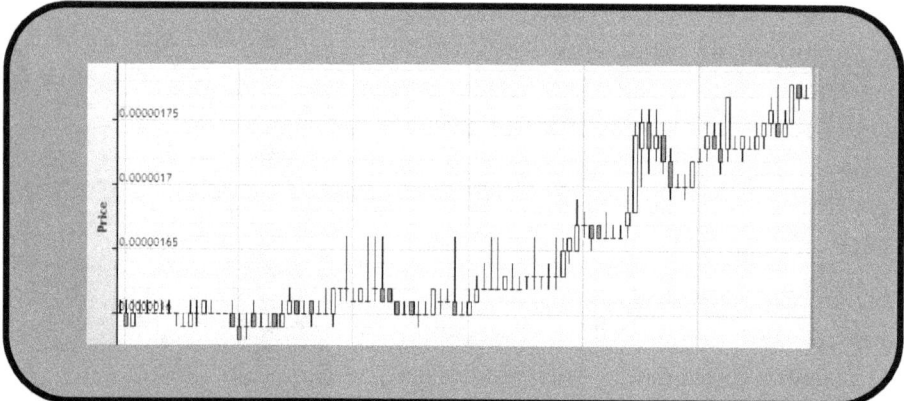

On the 11th of February, BTC38 initiated active trading of Dogecoin (DOGE/CNY). It is one of the most popular exchanges for Dogecoin in China. User "otakupcgamer" on Reddit described it as the Chinese equivalent of Cryptsy.

On the same day, user "Lubliana777" at 16:26:31 UTC announced that Newaltex had added Dogecoin to their exchange platform :

> "Dogecoin and Ultracoin were added to the exchange.
>
> https://www.newaltex.com/exchange/doge_btc
> https://www.newaltex.com/exchange/utc_btc"

On the 12th of February, the all time high market capitalisation of the year 2014 was reached at about $94 million. In doing so, it surpassed that of Peercoin and so became the third highest cryptocurrency in terms of market capitalisation on www.coinmarketcap.com. Taking into account Ripple (a pre-mined coin), it reached fourth position on this site.

According to www.cryptocoincharts.info, the Bitcoin Satoshi values of one unit of DOGE account and daily trading volumes on this day were:

	Price	Low	Open	Close	High	Volume (BTC)
Coined Up	275	251	270	280	350	161.606
Cryptsy	278	259	288	268	289	314.867
Coins-e	268.5	254	269	268	300	109.141
Vircurex	271.5	---	263	280	296	384.147
Bter	282	260	280	284	295	1404.14

On the 13th of February, Bittrex, a cryptocurrency exchange based in Seattle, Washington, USA, listed Dogecoin ready for trading. On this day, the exchange began operations in beta testing mode. Fifteen days later, twelve cryptocurrencies and twenty one trading pairs were initially made available besides Dogecoin as trading went live.

One day later, the average block reward halved for the first time from 500,000 DOGE to 250,000 DOGE at block number 100,001. At this time, approximately 50 billion DOGE had been mined.

Block #100,000 (Reward 348,118.17752744) Feb 14th 2014 at 02:59:41 AM UTC

Block #100,001 (Reward 191,608.02006203) Feb 14th 2014 at 03:00:22 AM UTC

On the 17th of February, the Dogechain (Dogecoin blockchain) forked (multiple blockchains). It was suspected that some mining pools were operating on the wrong blockchain. Users were advised to not to send any Dogecoin until the problem had been fixed. Developers were quick to respond to the issue during which time Jackson Palmer ("ummjackson" on Reddit) posted the following:

"This doesn't make sense—1.4.* and 1.5 would be hitting identical blockchains. If any fork has occurred, it's because a pool has used a modified version of the source code, or something pre-1.4.

Dogechain and the multiple nodes I've tested are all on the same blockchain, and I'm not observing any issues. /u/GlennMR, are you seeing any actual issues here?

I need to sleep (it's nearly 1am) but the key here is to not panic.
Make sure you're running the latest 1.5.1 client, do a resync and stay calm."

As a result of the fork in the Dogechain, version 1.5.2 of the wallet client was released. Jackson Palmer posted this release on github on the 17th of February:

"This minor release implements a checkpoint to ensure clients are on the correct blockchain, following a recent pre-1.5 fork that was created.

Updating is not mandatory, but highly recommended.
Do not run any pre-1.5 version of Dogecoin, as you may end up on the incorrect fork."

The Dogecoin community on Reddit were made aware of version 1.5.2 on the same day at 23:33:18 UTC by user "42points".

On the 19th of February, an exchange called MintPal initiated the DOGE/BTC pair for live trading. On the official MintPal Twitter page (@MintPalExchange), the following tweet was posted:

"We're back online, and what's that? Oh yes, we've just added a market for Dogecoin DOGE/BTC :)

https://www.mintpal.com/market/DOGE/BTC"

On the following day, Dogecoin went live on another cryptocurrency exchange called Kraken. According to its official Twitter page, it is based in San Francisco, California, USA. After several months of testing, the exchange moved from beta testing to being fully operational on the 9th of September 2013. Also, on the official Kraken Bitcointalk thread, DOGE went live at 3:00 PST to be precise.

Also on the same day, Comkort announced the inclusive of DOGE before going live. It was an exchange based in Estonia. According to its official Twitter Page, it began promotion and technical development back on the 14th of January 2014:

"Welcome! We launched promotional website of Cryptocoin Exchange Comkort http://comkort.com/ Development is underway, opening soon!"

It ceased trading operations on the 1st of July 2015. Users of the exchange then had an additional three weeks to withdraw their coins from there.

As well as Bitcoin and Litecoin being the cryptocurrencies of choice to trade against other coins, Dogecoin began to emerge as the third option. Some exchanges had opened up pairs which made it possible to trade numerous other coins against Dogecoin. Coined Up and Cryptorush were examples of this. Primecoin used to be the third coin to directly trade against on Cryptsy before Ripple was implemented.

On the 22nd of February, an exchange based in Brazil called useCryptos began to offer Dogecoin as a trading option.

On the 27th of February, Ben Doernberg (a former head of the Dogecoin Foundation) appeared on Fox News in a segment called "Fox On Reddit: Dogecoin, the virtual currency with a heart of gold". Ben Doernbeg said that the Dogecoin Subreddit is the core of the community. Other topics discussed were the Jamaican Bobsleigh Team, the Dogecoin Foundation and what the coin can purchase.

In the space of nearly three months, many cryptocurrency exchanges had added Dogecoin. There were also other means of acquiring the coin. Besides their corresponding website URL's, some of these were:

CoinedUp: https://coinedup.com/OrderBook?market=DOGE&base=BTC
Cryptsy: https://www.cryptsy.com/markets/view/132
Coins-E: https://www.coins-e.com/exchange/DOGE_BTC/
Vircurex: https://vircurex.com/welcome/index?alt=doge&base=btc
Bter: https://bter.com/trade/doge_btc
CoinEX: https://coinex.pw/trade/doge_btc
Poloniex: https://poloniex.com/exchange#btc_doge
Vault of Satoshi - USD/CAD to Dogecoin and back: https://www.vaultofsatoshi.com/
BTC38: http://www.btc38.com/trade.html?btc38_trade_coin_name=doge
Newaltex: https://www.newaltex.com/exchange/doge_btc
Bittrex: https://bittrex.com/Market/Index?MarketName=BTC-DOGE
MintPal: https://www.mintpal.com/market/DOGE/BTC
Buy, Sell, and Trade (ad hoc): http://doges.org/index.php?board=3.0
Buy and sell (ad hoc): http://www.reddit.com/r/dogemarket
Dogecoin marketplace: http://dogelist.com/
PMToCoins - Buy coins with Fiat: www.pmtocoins.com
Doge Marketplace - Ebay like site for DogeCoins: http://www.stuffcoins.com/doge/
Crypto Marketplace - Craigslist like site featuring DogeCoins: http://cryptomarketplace.net/

Other events which occurred in the month of February were:

- On the 1st of February, Swisscex added Dogecoin to their exchange.

- The total number of Dogecoin mined surpassed 40 billion on the 2nd of February. Also on this day, the number of subscribers of the /r/dogecoin Subreddit surpassed 50,000 (recorded as 50,659).

- On the 4th of February, user "/u/zimonitrome" won the "Dogecoin Hype Video Competition", so received 374,277 DOGE (60% of the prize fund) as winnings. The video was titled "Đ is for Đogecoin" (see below for video link).

- AllCoin (an exchange) added DOGE/BTC on the 5th of February.

- On the 17th of February, it was reported that Jack Palmer had rejected offers worth about $500,000 from at least two venture capitalist firms.

- At some point in February, a student got caught mining Dogecoin on Harvard's computers.

- During the month, an East London Burger Stall was accepting Dogecoin as payment.

NASCAR DRIVER JOSH WISE
SPONSORSHIP
MARCH 2014

I.   Dogecoin version 1.6 wallet client released.

II.   Doge4water fundraising target of 40,000,000 DOGE successfully reached.

III.   Hard fork of the blockchain at block number 145,000.

IV.   Sponsorship of Nascar Driver Josh Wise began.

V.   67.8Million DOGE (~$55,000) raised for Nascar driver Josh Wise.

On the first day of March, an article was published titled "Top 100 digital currencies by social media presence" on the site www.crypt.la (http://crypt.la/2014/03/01/top-100-digital-currencies-by-social-media-presence/). The article listed many popular cryptocurrencies in order of their "social strength" on Facebook, Reddit and Twitter. In this instance, the most popular Twitter page or Facebook group for each coin was adopted to note how many people were following. Dogecoin was listed in second position with the corresponding number of followers:

•   Facebook — 58,832; Reddit — 68,189; Twitter — 80,800.

In total, this gave Dogecoin 207,791. Bitcoin unsurprisingly topped the table at 410,184. It is often said a cryptocurrency is as strong as the community that supports and participates in it.

On the 4th of March at 00:46:10 UTC, a user called "ericnakagawa" on Reddit announced the Dogecoin Foundation's next goal. Their goal was to raise 40 million DOGE (~$50,000 at the time) via a partnership with charity:water (a New York City-based non-profit entity) to build two water wells in Kenya. A specific domain at www.doge4water.org was created in order to promote the charity campaign. On this website, their quoted goal was:

> "As part of our "Doge 4 Water" campaign, we're hoping to raise 40 million DOGE by "World Water Day" Saturday March 22, 2014 (to be converted to current value in USD)."
>
> Official donation wallet address: DNfFHTUZ4kkXPnoYUvgt6BGVwonEFB1b2i

After one week, about 16.3 million DOGE had been raised. A quote from fund raiser organiser Eric Nakagawa on the 11th of March was:

> "[It's a] super crazy goal. [...] If we don't hit the goal, it doesn't matter, if we can hit at least $20k, which I think is very, very likely, it will solve problems for hundreds of people."

On the 12th of March, an important wallet client update was released. Jack Palmer initially said the following on github:

> "Note: This is a mandatory update as it involves a hard fork of the network. Please make sure you are running 1.6 to ensure that you're on the correct blockchain and not at risk of losing your DOGE
>
> As per block 145k, the network will hardfork to adopt a new difficulty retargeting algorithm."

From block number 145,000, a few changes to the network protocol would kick in. Firstly, the block reward would no longer be random, but alter to being a static 250,000 DOGE per block until the next halving. Secondly, the difficulty re-targeting algorithm called DigiShield would become operational. Before this block, the difficulty re-targeted every 4 hours.

On the 15th of March 17:56:45 UTC, user "agx.io" notified the community on the official Bitcointalk thread that DOGE/BTC was active. Eleven trading pairs were initially available (free trading) including DOGE/BTC, RIC/BTC, BC/BTC, VTC/BTC, DGB/BTC, USDE/BTC, NOBL/BTC, MAX/BTC, LTC/BTC, LEAF/BTC, and AUR/BTC:

> "DOGE/BTC is LIVE on agx.io!
>
> Trade FREE during our Beta period!
>
> - The Austin Global Team
>
> Find us at:
> agx.io
> bitcointalk.org/index.php?topic=507474; bitcointalk handles: "agx.io," "AustinGlobal"
> twitter.com/AustinGlobalX; austinglobal.tumblr.com"

Austin Global Exchange

On the following day, the fund raising campaign to raise money for two wells in Kenya at www.doges4water.org reached its 40,000,000 DOGE target. A 14,000,000 tip (~$11,000) was sent by an individual via Twitter. Going by the name of "Hood" (@savethemhood) on this social media platform, he tweeted:

> "@tipdoge tip @Doge4water 14000000 may we all drink water. Let the wealthy fill your cup. #savethemhood"

At the time, it was the largest donation (tip) ever sent directly through a single tweet. It is unknown whether any individual or group has given more by this method since it happened. As a consequence of this donation, over one third of the target came from this mysterious member of the Dogecoin community.

He/she had used the automated Twitter-based Dogecoin Tipbot.

Block #144,999 (Reward 384,843.02) March 17th 2014 at 10:13:47 PM UTC

Block #145,000 (Reward 250,000) March 17th 2014 at 10:17:59 PM UTC

On the 17th of March, a hard fork of the blockchain occurred. As can be seen above, the block reward changed to a static 250,000 DOGE at which it would remain until block number 200,000.

Two days later, KTN News in Kenya reported the story of the Doge4water campaign to help build two water wells in Kenya. A total of about 2.5 million Shillings in Kenya's currency had now been donated (~40 million DOGE or ~$30,000). Thousands of people from the community had helped to make this a reality.

Not long after Doge4water, the community were quick to initiate another online fundraising campaign. Sponsorship of a car to race in a Nascar race had begun. On the 19th of March, a tweet was created by @SBNation:

"This Dogecoin car could be racing in NASCAR soon. sbn.to/1gaAClp "

A community member called Denis Pavel (a 16 year old Nascar fan) had noticed a Nascar driver without sponsorship called Josh Wise. By utilising the generosity of the Dogecoin community, he proposed the idea to raise the necessary funds in order to help Josh Wise. News reached Josh Wise who sent the following tweet:

> "Wow thanks for the support! Let's make it happen RT @Denis_Pavel:
>
> @Josh_Wise The Dogecoin Community and I are fundraising to sponsor you!"

In turn, this would be great advertising for the coin. It would increase awareness of Dogecoin, and cryptocurrency in general, in front of an audience of millions.

On the 20th of March at 02:58:50 UTC , user "futile-resistance" posted the links:

> "Yup, Moolah is gathering the donations on reddit.
> They're up to about 4 million doge so far.
>
> Here's the fiat donation page:
> http://www.youcaring.com/other/dogecoin-r-nascar-josh-wise-sponsorship/152173
>
> Here's the address:
> http://dogechain.info/address/DJ3fKdN6bfVeLKF6eLBbn5w3SMpRxbfKvE
>
> and here's the thread:
> http://www.reddit.com/r/dogecoin/comments/20t9pd/
> reddit_wants_to_wrap_a_nascar_in_dogecoin/"

A couple of hours later, user "futile-resistance" decided to create a new Bitcointalk thread titled "Dogecoin reddit sponsoring Nascar driver Josh Wise". He said:

> "Alrighty, I created a new thread.
>
> https://bitcointalk.org/index.php?topic=523121.msg5796884#msg5796884
>
> Would love to see it happen."

Five days later at 20:05:31 UTC, user "Predseda4D" said:

> "ÐOGE for NASCAR is funded.
>
> http://www.reddit.com/r/dogecoin/comments/21c5xq/doge4nascar_is_funded/
>
> http://www.sbnation.com/lookit/2014/3/25/5546138/nascar-doge-dogecoin-talladega-reddit
>
> https://twitter.com/Josh_Wise/status/446464103973130243
>
> Such Vroom. Very speed! "

In the space of five days, the community had successfully raised a grand total of about 67.8 million DOGE. At the time, this roughly equated to $55,000. This figure meant that Josh Wise (#98) would be racing in the Aaron's 499 in Talladega, Alabama, USA on the 2nd-4th of May 2014. The fundraising organiser was Kevin Dusenberry. He said:

> "This is awesome. A great thanks to the community and everyone who has donated. First we'll win NASCAR and then we race off to the moon!"
>
> http://doge4nascar.com/
> http://www.reddit.com/.../comme.../21c5xq/doge4nascar_is_funded/
> http://www.sbnation.com/.../nascar-doge-dogecoin-talladega-re...

Two days after the funds had been raised, Josh Wise was interviewed via Skype on "Fox On Reddit" by Gary Gastelu. Josh Wise described the Dogecoin community as passionate and amazing. He had also personally participated in discussions with them on the Dogecoin Subreddit. The video was uploaded at:

> https://www.youtube.com/watch?feature=player_embedded&v=ER4fsH3Ldw4

On the 29th of March, a post on the official Dogecoin Facebook page listed the possible ways to get in contact with Dogecoin developers and the team:

"Remember that you can reach us here on facebook at this page (Dogecoin) or this group: www.fb.com/groups/DogeCoinGroup
On reddit: http://www.reddit.com/r/dogecoin

per E-Mail at info@dogecoin.com. Or follow the Dogecoin people on twitter:

@dogecoin   @jacksonpalmer   @bendoernberg   @oskar_mix   @KasperRudstedt
@ericnakagawa1   @joshmohland1   @billymarkus"

Other events which occurred in the month of March were:

- On the 7th of March, the co-founder of Vault of Satoshi, Ryan, announced it would cease trading for USA based customers. It was due to a lack of co-operation from FinCEN regulations in the USA.

- On the 13th of March, international payment processing platform GoCoin announced plans to include Dogecoin as a payment option on their site.

- On the 14th of March, Dogecoin began to trade on CoinMarket.io. Both DOGE/BTC and DOGE/USD trading pairs were initiated.

- On the 18th of March, 100 days had passed since block number one was timestamped to the blockchain. A video was uploaded to YouTube by user "QuantumDesignsHD" to celebrate this milestone.

- Jackson Palmer and Josh Mohland attended CoinSummit in San Francisco at Yerba Buena Center for the Arts on the 26th of March. They both spoke at the event. Other speakers included Charlie Lee, Brian Armstrong (CEO of Coinbase), Nicolas Cary (CEO of Blockchain) and Marc Andreessen.

- On the 27th of March, the exchange called OpenEx closed its doors.

- On the 30th of March, the DOGE/USD trading pair was added to Cryptsy.

DOGECOIN CONFERENCE (DOGECON)
HELD IN SAN FRANCISCO
APRIL 2014

I. Dogecoin added to GoCoin (an international payment processing platform).

II. Charlie Lee of Litecoin recommended merge mining with Dogecoin.

III. An official update from Jack Palmer posted on Reddit.

IV. First Dogecoin conference (Dogecon) held in San Francisco.

V. Block reward reduced from 250,000 DOGE to 125,000 DOGE.

On the first day of April, an international payment processing platform posted the following tweet about its most recent addition:

> "No April Fools in @SiliconBeach_LA ... #Dogecoin now live as a payment option on the @GoCoin platform #Bitcoin http://www.gocoin.com"

Two days later, Max Keller (Langerhans) posted his first github Dogecoin wallet update called "Dogecoin Core 1.7 Alpha". He emphasised that this was an early release of the client (hard-coded to only work with testnet). He said:

> "Dogecoin Core 1.7 is a complete re-architecture of Dogecoin, changing from using the Litecoin client as its base, to Bitcoin 0.9. It's still Dogecoin, same Scrypt PoW algorithm, same reward schedule, but there's a lot of changes under the hood."

On the 5th of April at 22:25:49 UTC, a user called "killerstorm" posted content in the Bitcoin Subreddit (www.reddit.com/r/Bitcoin) titled:

> "Most alt-coins are NOT secure enough, they exist only for entertainment and speculation"

Charlie Lee ("coblee"), the founder of Litecoin (LTC), replied to this thread about nine hours later. He proposed merge mining of Dogecoin and Litecoin:

> "I have actually suggested this to Jackson Palmer and he seemed intrigued by the idea. We'll see if he agrees.
> Litecoin and Dogecoin merged mined would be beneficial to both coins.
>
> I've known pretty much since before I created Litecoin that in order to survive, you can't compete with Bitcoin for miners. So you'd need to be mined on a different class of hardware. I believe this fact will be pretty clear when ASICs for Scrypt becomes widely available."

Simply put, merge mining allows miners to simultaneously mine more than one blockchain. It helps to increase the hash (the overall processing power committed by miners in order to successfully find blocks) of the participant coins without effecting the underlying characteristics of each of those coins. Therefore, the network protocol of Dogecoin would be more secure and more resistant to a possible future 51% attack.

A significant proportion of the Dogecoin community voiced their opposition or held reservations about this idea. It was their preference to keep Dogecoin independent of other cryptocurrencies at a technical level.

Nevertheless, discussions were underway. A decision on the matter would require detailed technical analysis by the developers as well as input from members of the community.

On the 8th of April at 04:48:22 UTC, Jack Palmer posted an official update:

"What a busy few weeks it's been - I've recently moved from Sydney over to San Francisco so inbetween working my day job, attending CoinSummit and gathering rocket fuel for Dogecoin, I've been trying to settle in to a new city.

There have been a bunch of a shibes who have reached out to me these past few weeks, and if I haven't been able to reply it's been purely because of how busy I've been (I try to reply to all emails, so sorry if I've missed you!). To help answers these questions, I wanted to do a quick check-in here on Reddit just to update everyone on where my head is at, and where I see Dogecoin going (on it's moon journey, of course!)."

This update was posted on the Dogecoin Subreddit on which Palmer gave his view on three topics (The Dogecoin Foundation, core development and merge mining).

Jack took the opportunity to praise "/u/Laika1954" (Liam Butler) for his efforts in establishing the Dogecoin Foundation. It was Liam who helped promote the charity events called Dogesled and Doge4kids. Unfortunately, Liam moved on, so Jack stepped in temporarily to update the website and help organise the doge4water initiative alongside Erik Nakagawa. Jack was pleased to say that Ben Doernberg and Eric Nakagawa were the current heads of the foundation.

In terms of network protocol development, Jack and Billy were the initial developers. However, as time progressed, they needed more experienced help in order to further the project. Many contributors, including "/u/lleti", helped to release version 1.6 (12th March). Jack announced that Max Keller (/u/langer_hans) had been appointed as the lead developer of Dogecoin. He had developed the code of the Dogecoin Android Wallet called "dogecoinj". He had also released "Dogecoin 1.7.0 Alpha 1" five days ago (his first github Dogecoin wallet update).

Jack met Charlie Lee at the recent CoinSummit event in San Franciso (26th March). They discussed the issue of merge mining and the future of cryptocurrencies. Jack was unconvinced that merge mining was appropriate at this time, but was open to its implementation in the future if conditions required it.

Photo by Biz Carson/Gigaom

On the 16th of April, an upcoming conference to be held in San Francisco on the 25th of April was announced. Organised by "Follow the Coin" (a FinTech news site) in partnership with the Dogecoin Foundation, it would be an event to celebrate the history of the coin so far. Guests already invited to the event (Dogecon) were Charlie Lee (Litecoin founder), David Dvorak (Dogetipbot co-founder), Eric Nakagawa (Doge4water organiser) and Andreas Antonopoulous (Author of 'Mastering Bitcoin'). Jackson Palmer (the event headliner) was quoted as saying:

"Dogecoin is based, at its core, around a passionate community of users who are a fine example of how generosity and light-heartedness can prevail on the often mean-spirited internet. Dogecon is an extension of that community drive, and my hope is that it'll bring together shibes for a night of crypto-education, discussion and a heap of fun."

One day later, a Chinese exchange called BTC100 announced that Dogecoin trading (DOGE/CNY) would commence in two days time on the 19th of April:

"Through our careful study and selection, we decided on the line Dogecoin transactions and advance open recharge. Dogecoin recharge will open at 19:00 on April 17. Recharge the waiting for you to come and collect prizes Oh!

Dogecoin transaction will be opened at 10:00 on the 19th."

On the 22nd of April, a wallet client update was released called "Dogecoin 1.7.0 Beta 2". It fixed a bug in the code found in the last update.

Three days later, the day of the anticipated conference in San Francisco arrived. As mentioned previously, there were recognisable speakers who spoke to an enthusiastic audience of Dogecoin supporters. A total of about 2,000 people attended in person or through live stream. Jackson Palmer was the first person to speak on stage after being introduced by Matt Schlicht and Tina Hui of "Follow The Coin". During his speech, Jack highlighted some statistics to date:

~75,000 subshibers to www.reddit.com/r/dogeocin
>~$150,000 in DOGE tipped using /u/dogetipbot
>~$100,000 raised so far for officially known charities
~166,000 Twitter followers on the official Dogecoin Twitter page
~61,000 Facebook likes on the official Dogecoin Facebook page

~3.5 million visits to the official Dogecoin website at www.dogecoin.com

Jack said he was surprised how far Dogecoin had come in a short space of time.

Jackson Palmer, co-founder of Dogecoin, speaks at Dogecon on Friday, April 25.
Photo by Biz Carson/Gigaom

On the 27th of April at 17:22:05 UTC, user "futile-resistance" said:

"The dogecar is done being painted:

The reddit will also be sponsoring an MMA fighter as well.
Here's the info on that:
http://www.reddit.com/r/dogecoin/comments/23d3qi/
spikedoge_sponsor_austin_moon4_big_updates_moolah/

Moolah will be handling the donations."

Members of the community helped to design the wrap as seen above via crowdsourcing. Only one week remained until the race at Talladega in Alabama, USA. Josh Wise was quoted as saying:

"Watching this whole thing come to life from the beginning has been crazy. The support of the Reddit and Dogecoin community is just mind boggling, and now we are sitting here with the Dogecoin community's "Moon Rocket"! If it's as fast on the track as it looks we will have a great weekend at Talladega."

Also on the 27th of April, a post was published on the official DOGE Facebook page:

On the 28th of April, the second halving of the block reward happened (see below).

Other events which occurred in the month of April were:

- The official Dogecoin Bitcointalk thread surpassed 1,000 pages of comments or replies on the 8th of April.

- On the 12th of April, v1.7.0 beta 1 of the wallet client was released.

- On the 17th of April, the first issue of the Dogecoin Magazine titled "Very Much Wow" was published. It contained news, interviews, entertainment and other interesting trivia. It was issue number one for May 2014.

Block #199,999 (Reward 250,000) April 28th 2014 at 03:30:39 PM UTC

Block #200,000 (Reward 125,000) April 28th 2014 at 03:32:20 PM UTC

JOSH WISE RACED AT TALLADEGA

MAY 2014

I.   Doge4Housing goal of 11 million DOGE achieved in less than 24 hours.

II. Josh Wise in the DogeCar finished 20th at Talladega in Alabama, USA.

III. Dogecoin Foundation completely dismantled ready for elections.

IV. Kevin Rose had a conversation with Jackson Palmer.

V.   Dogecoin version 1.7 wallet client released.

On the outset of the month, the Dogecoin community were, yet again, helping to raise funds for a worthwhile cause. The latest campaign was to raise 11 million Dogecoin for five Minnesota families with critically ill or seriously injured children in hospital. These families were struggling to simultaneously keep a roof over their heads and afford medical costs. In less than 24 hours, the goal for Doge4Housing was achieved on the 1st of May. Jack Palmer was quoted as saying:

"It's always sad to see families displaced from their homes due to hefty medical bills, and Doge4Housing is a great campaign aimed to help those families out there currently struggling to focus on the most important thing -- their child's health -- while keeping a roof over their heads.
Spare Key is a great cause, and I'm glad that the Dogecoin community can help rally behind it."

On the second day of the month, Josh Wise drove the #98 Dogecoin Car (dubbed the "Dogecar" — "racegod" backwards) at the Talladega practice session. During the Fox Sport television channel commentary, Darrell Waltrip said:

> "I'm gonna go on the old Google machine and figure this Dogecoin out"

Josh Wise qualified for the main event at Talladega, Alabama. As a result, he had booked his place in the main event on the 4th of May. It would be televised on Fox at 13:00 EST in front of millions of Nascar supporters.

At Aaron's 499 race at Talladega Superspeedway, Josh Wise finished in 20th position. During the race, he skilfully evaded two major crashes.

Also on the 4th of May, Howard from www.dailydoge.org, wrote an article titled "5 Crazy Fun Facts About Dogecoin". These were:

1. "Back in February of 2014, Jackson Palmer (co-founder of Dogecoin), declined a $500,000 investment offer from Australian venture capitalists trying to cash in on the Dogecoin phenomenon."

2. "The legendary house music producer Deadmau5 is reportedly an undercover Shibe himself. Back in January, Deadmau5 revealed publicly in a Tweet that he will be accepting Dogecoin."

3. "The Shiba Inu is actually considered a difficult breed in terms of temperament. During times of stress or extreme joy, the Shiba Inu is also known to emit a shrill "shiba scream" which is described to be similar to a human female scream."

4. "The Dogecoin community is home to a number of anonymous tippers who are hell bent on donating large amounts of Dogecoin. The mysterious silentShibe is notorious for silently tipping thousands of dollars worth of Dogecoin — all without a peep. Don't forget the mysterious SaveThemHood who also lurks in the shadows yet contributes thousands of dollars in free donations to both the community and various charities."

5. "The popular phrase "to the moon" is often associated with the Dogecoin community; however, it actually first gained traction within the Bitcoin world and was then later adopted by Dogecoin."

On the 6th of May, Josh Wise was interviewed by Ashley Dvorkin on "Fox on Reddit". Josh Wise described how he felt the race went. He was very happy about how the Dogecoin community, particularly on Reddit, had helped promote Nascar to a wider audience. Any future Dogecoin sponsorship was not ruled out.

On the following day, an important Dogecoin Foundation announcement was published on Reddit by user "foundationelection" at 13:34:28 UTC. In this announcement, it was made clear that the original Dogecoin Foundation had been dismantled. The original members Jack Palmer, Ben Doernberg and Eric Nakagawa stood down. They were in the process of creating a new and improved foundation by holding fair and unbiased elections (17 available positions). Their goal was:

> "The Foundation will exist as a separate entity from the Dogecoin community and yet, at the same time, be beholden to it, for you are the reason that it exists. Moderators of /r/dogecoin can not also be members of the foundation or vice versa. Elected members of the Foundation will need to contact moderation team for sticky's, flairs, etc."

Members of the community were encouraged to participate in this process. All information attaining to ongoing discussions and the choices made were disclosed to those who wished to see it. Ultimately, they wanted the new Dogecoin Foundation to truly reflect the community.

Five days later, lead developer "langerhans" released v1.7.0 of the Dogecoin wallet client on github. It changed the code base from that derived from Litecoin to Bitcoin 0.9.

On the 12th of May at 17:42:47 UTC, user "futile-resistance" said:

> "Josh Wise is in the top 10 for the Sprint Fan Vote, if he wins he'll be driving the Dogecar in the All Star Race.
>
> https://twitter.com/MissSprintCup/status/465903075832918016
>
> If you've got time, maybe throw in a retweet. Pretty exciting if he wins."

Jack Palmer was interviewed by Kevin Rose in a video titled "Very Foundation, Much Wow: A Conservation With Dogecoin's Jackson Palmer". It was uploaded on the 12th of May. In the video, Jack discussed his early life in Sydney, his work at Adobe and where he envisages to see cryptocurrency in five years time. On the issue of Bitcoin, he was quoted as saying:

"The way to win more people's hearts and build adoption is to unpeg from get-rich-quick schemes. Unfortunately Bitcoin today is sold incorrectly. Telling friends and family, 'you're going to get rich off bitcoin' is completely underselling. Bitcoin is a fast, decentralized way to conduct payments online without transaction fees. We're revolutionizing the future way that people trade."

On the 13th of May at 17:24:19 UTC, user "coinnext " said:

"Coinnext Exchange added DOGE. Trade DOGE/BTC
https://coinnext.com/trade/DOGE/BTC"

On the 16th of May, Josh Wise won the "Sprint Fan Vote". It meant that it would be his first time participating in the 2014 Sprint All Star Race on the 17th of May 2014. Congratulations came from @NASCARONFOX on Twitter:

@Josh_Wise on winning #SprintFanVote: "Man, that's unreal. I can't believe that. It's amazing .. Thanks to everyone at Reddit & #dogecoin"

On the 17th of May, a Dogecoin party occurred at the Shilo Inn, Airport Way in Portland, USA. The event was organised by Josh Mohland.

Discussion at the end of the month centred on the future security and sustainability of the blockchain. Members of the community suggested whether changing the timestamping algorithm to PoS or PoW/PoS would benefit the coin in the long term. Evidence existed that the hash (the overall processing power committed by miners towards successfully solving and finding blocks) had been decreasing over time, especially after each of the first two block reductions on the 14th of February and the 28th of April. According to www.bitinfocharts.com, the average hash (GHash/s) decreased from 124.09 on the 13th of February to 77.71 two days later. Also, it decreased from 67.65 on the 28th of April to 49.92 the following day:

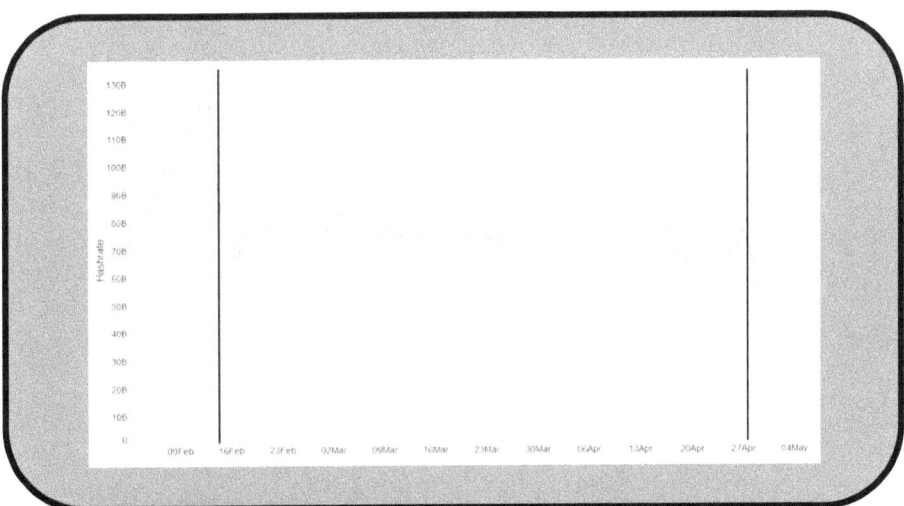

Other events which occurred in the month of May were:

- On the 6th of May, a used car dealership and repair shop in southern Wisconsin called Cartopia began to accept Dogecoin as a means of payment.

- On the 17th of May, Josh Wise finished 15th in the NASCAR Sprint All-Star Race in Charlotte, North Carolina, USA. This time he drove a Chevrolet.

- On the 25th of May, a contest began to design a Facebook cover photo for the official Dogecoin Facebook page.

- Tina Hui of "Follow The Coin" created several videos based on Dogecoin.

COMMUNITY QUESTION & ANSWERS WITH DOGECOIN CO-FOUNDER JACKSON PALMER

JUNE 2014

I. Dogecoin Tipping App approved on Facebook.

II. Dogecoin began trading on HitBTC, Kingcoiny and mcxNOW.

III. Three million DOGE successfully raised for CESHEO.

IV. Dogecoin version 1.7.1 wallet client released.

V. Jackson Palmer severing ties with Dogecoin community on Reddit.

In the space of one week short of six months, Dogecoin had gone from a "joke" to one of the largest (if not the largest) cryptocurrency communities. Dogecoin had now established itself as one of the major cryptocurrencies. For some time, doubt had arisen in the community whether the coin could sustain itself in terms of its popularity, functionality and security. Questions were posed to the co-creator of Dogecoin, Jack Palmer, by the community. Twelve of these can be found in the appendix of this book on pages 131 to 137.

On the 1st of June, the price of one DOGE unit of account went from a low of 54 Bitcoin Satoshi to 74 Bitcoin Satoshi on Cryptsy.

On the 3rd of June, an exchange called HitBTC announced that Dogecoin had been listed ready for active trading. It was not until two weeks later that active trading of DOGE commenced on that platform.

On the 6th of June, an announcement was made. Facebook had approved the "Doge Tipping App", developed by Alejandro Caballero, on the previous day. User "lavacaballero" at 03:13:10 UTC posted the following:

"Some days ago we got The Doge Tipping App being the first of its kind. Some adjustments where made during the review, but it was already approved.

When we submitted the Doge-only app, the Multicoin Tipping App was also submitted. But we needed to change several things to have it finally approved, which happened a few minutes ago.

It's been a long road. Especially with the Multicoin Tipping App -which also supports Dogecoin-.

Now we're dragging some fellow coins into the big field in the most pure spirit of shibing.

Now our work with Facebook is complete. We'll go back to finishing the universal platform to allow tipping on Wordpress, Drupal, Joomla, Xenforo, PHPBB and a big etcetera :D

PS: Cheers to all of you guys that never stopped believing in our work and a big hug to "Jon", who posted this on our support forum:

http://www.whitepuma.net/dogetipping/forum/index.php?id=17"

On the 8th of June, the trading pair DOGE/BTC went live on the exchange called mcxNOW. From the beginning, users could not deposit less than 10,000 DOGE at a time. It was an exchange that offered interest (fluctuated with trade volume) on deposited coins. Only about ten cryptocurrencies were available to trade on there.

The following was tweeted by @mcxNOWexchange on that day:

"#mcxNOW 2.5 live. Now with #dogecoin and significant codebase improvements. Already beating #cryptsy volume. #Bitcoin #BTC"

After a few hours of trading on mcxNOW, the volume of the Dogecoin trading pair was almost 200 BTC. It was an exchange coded in C++.

Six days later, three million DOGE were successfully raised for CESHEO (Cambodia English School of Higher Education Organisation). It provides a free education to more than 750 Cambodian children who otherwise would not get an education. On their official website at http://www.ceshe.org/donate.html#dogecoin they say:

"After a successful fundraiser with dogecoin we will now be taking donations all year round to help our organisation. ... Our next project is to build a toilet at one of our schools."

On the 15th of June, lead developer "langerhans" released version 1.7.1 of the wallet client. At 19:09:55 UTC, the relevant post on Reddit was submitted:

"Hi Shibes!

We want to announce the release of Dogecoin Core 1.7.1. This is a security release.

Dogecoin Core 1.7.1 is built against OpenSSL 1.0.1h, released to close recently disclosed vulnerabilities, which could have an impact on the usage of RPC over SSL. If you use this feature, it is advised that you upgrade to 1.7.1 and OpenSSL 1.0.1h.

If you do not use RPC over SSL or don't even know what RPC is, you don't need to upgrade.

No other changes where made in this release.

If you are still using Dogecoin Core 1.6 and also use RPC over SSL in a publicly accessible manner, we advise you to upgrade to 1.7.1 or restrict the usage of RPC to your local controlled network.

Get it at http://dogecoin.com or compile it from https://github.com/dogecoin/dogecoin if you need to :) That's all, thanks :)

EDIT: The Mac version still shows 1.7.0. That's fine though as the OpenSSL version is still correct. Sorry if that lead to confusion."

On the 20th of June, it was reported that the average fiat value of one unit of DOGE had decreased to $0.000358, the lowest value per coin since January. Some members of the community thought the increasing number of other cryptocurrencies were diluting the value of the coin. However, others were more optimistic of a price rebound due to a strong community and tipping philosophy.

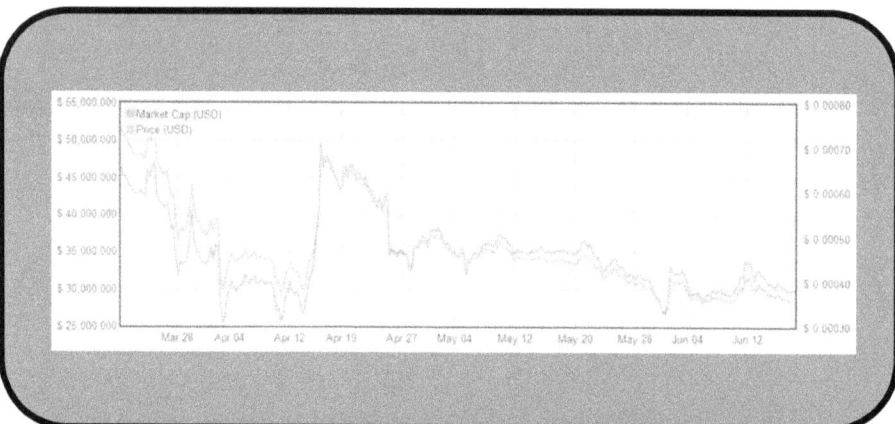

On the 24th of June, Jackson Palmer surprisingly unsubscribed from the Dogecoin Subreddit. It stemmed from a public argument between himself and Alex Green, the creator of the platform Moolah.io, over UltraPRO seeking trademark of DOGE. This dispute had been happening for the past few days. Jack said:

"Given that I just can't be bothered dealing with the massive amounts of hate you've somehow had directed at me though, in the past 24 hours, I'm going to step back and let you run this community here on Reddit from now on, which you obviously own. Unsubshibing. Peace."

Alex Green replied angrily:

"Really? Are you going to respond with that? That is ridiculously childish. You're being pissy because you no longer run the community. I never have, and I never will, and I will never want to. Personally, I will be very glad once you step back from this coin and let the community run it."

A significant number of people thought he had left the community altogether.

However, one day later, Jackson Palmer (@ummjackson) tweeted the following on his official Twitter account:

> "To clarify, I'm not leaving @dogecoin altogether - just staying away from /r/dogecoin on Reddit, which has gotten a little toxic. :)"

Taking into account the strong community presence of Dogecoin on Reddit, it was understandable how this confusion had come about. The vast majority of announcements and discussion were on that social media platform.

Other events which occurred in the month of June were:

- At the beginning of June, user "GlennMR" released the public beta of the online wallet on the official Dogecoin block explorer called DogeChain. It is similar to the model used at blockchain.info.

- On the 4th of June, an exchange called Kingcoiny initiated Dogecoin on their platform.

- On the 6th of June, Josh Mohland announced a Dogetipbot service update called Megatron. It increased the security and functionality of the tipping service by enabling approximately forty transactions per second.

- On the 13th of June, Bter opened several new direct USD trading pairs. These were for the coins Bitcoin, LiteCoin, NXT, DogeCoin, DarkCoin and CounterParty (XCP).

- An official Twitter account for the Dogecoin Foundation (@TheDogecoinFdn) was created on the 25th of June.

- On the 27th of June, Bobby Ong of CoinGecko wrote an article published on www.dailydoge.org. On this site, Dogecoin was ranked in second position with 87,878 subscribers on Reddit, 63,380 Facebook likes and 165,084 Twitter followers.

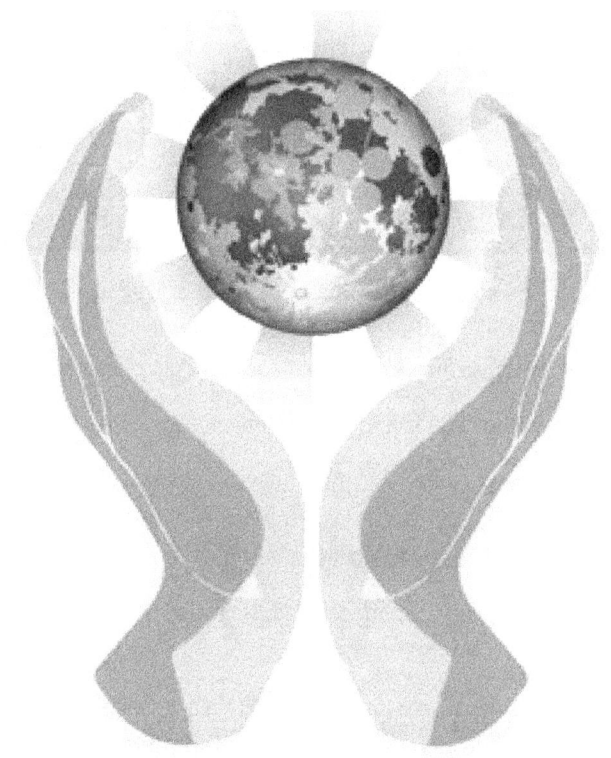

NEW DOGECOIN FOUNDATION

JULY 2014

I.   New Dogecoin Foundation established.

II.   Lowest fiat value of one DOGE during the last five to six months.

III.   Block reward reduced from 125,000 to 62,500 DOGE.

IV.   Charlie Lee brought up the issue of merge mining again.

V.   Tristan Winters of Bitcoin Magazine interviewed "Langerhans".

By means of continuous use of social media, predominantly Reddit, an important announcement was released on the opening day of July. A new Dogecoin Foundation had been formed consisting of five temporary board members (familiar names to the community). It would be their responsibility to create firm grounds after which a leadership election would happen within the next three months. Members of this new foundation were:

Felix von Drigalski, Jens Wiechers, Steven Hirschmann, Josh Mohland and Debbie Ballard.

Their first task was to publish a roadmap to inform the community of future objectives to be worked upon. Praise was given to all those in the community who had made this transition possible either in its legality or through helpful input.

On the 3rd of July, according to www.bitinfocharts.com, the value one unit of DOGE account stood at about $0.00022. This was the lowest average fiat valuation derived from BTC/USD and DOGE/BTC in during the last five to six months. On the day of its all time high market capitalisation, one DOGE was worth ~$0.00180. Most other cryptocurrencies had also decreased substantially over the same period. The table below shows the Bitcoin Satoshi values of one unit of DOGE account on the ten most popular cryptocurrencies on the 3rd of July:

	Price	Low	Open	Close	High	Volume (BTC)
Cryptsy	34.5	32	33	36	37	156.381
Bter	34.5	31	36	33	36	36.7187
MintPal	34.5	32	35	34	36	15.1991
Vircurex	36	32	37	35	52	8.6511
Kraken	34.5	29	35	34	37	2.96278
Poloniex	34.5	30	34	35	42	2.53072
Bittrex	35	32	35	35	36	1.93568
Coined Up	34	31	35	33	37	1.04311

source: www.cryptocoincharts.info

As is obvious above, over half the total daily trading volume on all exchanges existed on Cryptsy. Dogecoin still has substantial trading volume on this exchange at the time of publication of this book.

Concerning the price of Dogecoin, the co-creator of the coin called Jack Palmer said the following at the Dogecoin conference (Dogecon) in San Francisco back in April:

"I've said this a lot recently, but 1 DOGE = 1 DOGE. And what this means to those who are unaware, is that the viability of a digital currency shouldn't be pegged to what you can cash out in fiat currency form."

Block #299,999 (Reward 125,000) July 15th 2014 at 05:35:33 PM UTC

Block #300,000 (Reward 62,500) July 15th 2014 at 05:47:32 PM UTC

Twelve days later, the reward of each block generated halved for the fourth time.

On the 19th of July, Charlie Lee at the second North American Bitcoin Conference (TNABC) at McCormick Place in Chicago brought up the issue of merge mining once more. The Dogecoin community were still divided on whether to go ahead with it or not. Lee was quoted as saying:

"The Dogecoin development team needs to do something. Most people in the community actually don't understand the problem. The hashrate is so low that it's getting dangerous. It's getting to the point where anyone with a small ASIC farm can attack it."

On the penultimate day of July, Tristan Winters of Bitcoin Magazine interviewed the lead developer of Dogecoin called 'langerhans'. The transcript of this can be found in the appendix of this book on pages 139 to 144.

Other events which occurred in the month of July were:

- Snapcard, a money service business based in San Francisco, USA, incorporated Dogecoin. It is a service to allow users to buy goods/services on websites that do not accept cryptocurrencies. An announcement of its addition was made on the 1st of July on Reddit.

- On the 25th of July, 10 million DOGE were raised for Doge4eSports. It was an initiative to give highschoolers the opportunity to compete for Dogecoin.

- On the 29th of July, some users on the Dogecoin Freenode IRC Channel were witnessed recruiting others for the purposes of launching a 51% attack on the Dogecoin network. A 51% attack is possible when an entity (one person or group of people) controls over half the overall hash of the network. They can then successfully spend the same coins more than once.

VERSION 1.8 WALLET CLIENT RELEASED

AUGUST 2014

I.   Developers decided to go ahead with merge mining with Litecoin.

II.   Another cryptocurrency called Dogeparty launched.

III.   Josh Mohland interviewed by Jason Calacanis on "This Week In Startups".

IV.   An exchange called CEX.IO added Dogecoin.

V.   Mandatory Dogecoin version 1.8 wallet client released.

After lengthy discussions between members of the community, a decision was finally made regarding the method by which future Dogecoins would be mined. It had been obvious to many Shibes that the total processing power (hash), which secures the network protocol, had continued to decrease over the last few months. The developers wanted to safeguard the coin's future by going ahead with this change. A shift from Scrypt proof of work to Scrypt Auxiliary proof of work would occur. Howard (www.dailydoge.org) described this new timestamping method:

> "AuxPoW is essentially a form of (or pretty much is) merged mining.
> A Scrypt miner interested in mining Litecoin can now contribute the same hash to both the Litecoin and the Dogecoin blockchains.
> Likewise, the miner will collect rewards for both coins. Scrypt miners now have incentive to help secure the Dogecoin network without sacrificing their profits."

AUGUST 2014

On the 3rd of August, user "Dogecoin" at 15:22:35 UTC posted the following announcement on the official Dogecoin Bitcointalk thread regarding a future technical upgrade of the Dogecoin network protocol. This was also posted on the Dogecoin Subreddit eighteen seconds earlier:

"Today marks an important day in the history of Dogecoin. We are here to announce that we will enable the Dogecoin blockchain to accept auxiliary proof of work from other Scrypt chains. As you all know, we've been looking into a lot of options. AuxPoW has been on the table for quite some time now and has been recently again discussed at length.

We have also discussed many other options, some of them which are still highly theoretical, or just deemed to be in Alpha state. We didn't see them as viable for that exact reason. AuxPoW has been around in the crypto space for quite a while now. Our topmost priority has always been to provide a stable platform for the currency and its services and of course its users. We hope that with AuxPoW we can achieve that in a better way than what it currently is like. Our hashrate has been on a decline and we hope that we can gain more of it with the acceptance of proof of work from other chains.

Yes, this does mean that we are going to fork. The exact switchover is yet to be determined but will happen sooner than later. This post is here to announce it early enough for everyone to prepare for the update. The code is currently in the late testing stage and we are working on ironing out the last small issues.

We will also push a new branch to the [Github repo](https://github.com/dogecoin/dogecoin) called `1.8-dev` which has the AuxPoW switch on the testnet set for block 158,100 (Tomorrow 6:30 GMT). The updated branch will be available later today, so keep an eye on the repo if you're interested. This will be done to help pool operators test the mining on the AuxPoW enabled chain in preperation of the switch on the main chain. If you know how to compile the client, then you can certainly help us by trying it out and even mine a bit with a few KH on the testnet. What you need to know, if you already have the testnet chain synced, is to start the client with `-reindex` the first time you run 1.8. This should be automated for the final so the transition will be as smooth as possible.What this does not mean is that we're tying us to Litecoin. What we do is accepting Proof of Work from their miners if they happen to hit our difficulty target. But that is technical background stuff, which was explained several times before here. On that note, and I'm no economist, I also don't see that have any negative effect on the price, considering the amount of "dumped" coins would probably not change. Also, you as miners are not forced to mine Litecoin to get Dogecoin now. You can still mine at your current pools directly to the Dogecoin network.

98

The Android wallet and Multidoge will receive an update if needed.

I'll have to dig into this now

Please stay tuned for any updates. We'll be pushing them through all the channels.
Thanks everyone for their continued support!

-langer_hans

More on reddit here:
http://www.reddit.com/r/dogecoin/comments/2ci90m/
dogecoin_to_enable_auxpow_soon_all_infos_inside/"

Ten days later at 13:06:00 UTC, a Bitcointalk thread was created for a new coin called Dogeparty (XDP) titled "[ANN] Dogeparty, Counterparty for the Dogecoin blockchain! (official)". User "wendell" submitted the opening post. During a period of thirty days beginning on the 12th of August, it was possible for people to burn 1,000 Dogecoin to receive one Dogeparty (XDP) token.

On the 15th of August, a video was uploaded to YouTube titled "DogeTipBot is the cryptocurrency tipping tool taking reddit by storm". Filmed before this day, the host of "This Week In Startups" called Jason Calacanis interviewed Josh Mohland (co-creator of DogeTipBot). They both demonstrated to listeners how to tip Dogecoin on Reddit. They also discussed:

- Why would people want to tip others?

- Will DogeTipBot go mainstream in the future?

- Some of the charity campaigns Dogecoin raised funds for.

- Has any individual or business shown interest in investing money into DogeTipBot?

DogeTipBot had been active for about eight months. Josh Mohland mentioned that about 10% of all tips in DOGE are not accepted by recipients and about 28% of recipients who accept the tips tip DOGE back.

The corresponding description of the video was:

"This week, Jason talks to a pioneer in the Wild West of cryptocurrency. Eight months ago Josh Mohland created DogeTipBot, a tool for tipping with dogecoin on the internet. Since then, 70k users (and climbing) have gone to town gifting -- to each other for fun in fractions of pennies, and en masse for charity, building wells in Africa and sending the Jamaican bobsled team to the Olympics for $25k. You don't want to miss this conversation!"

Four days later at 19:30:34 UTC, user "langer_hans" posted the following update on Reddit. He said:

"Hey shibes!

Since we announced the switch to AuxPoW a lot of work has been done. Extensive testing, much coding, a bit of wow here and there ;)
Well, today we'd like to announce that the switch is planned to happen at block 371337

I projected this to be somewhere around 4:56:00 pm GMT |
Friday, September 12, 2014 (+- a few hours I guess)
The Core client is in a very good shape (If you want to test it right now and know how to compile use the 1.8-dev branch and hop on the testnet), dogecoinj implementation is done, which means Android and MultiDoge will be ready soon enough too.
We plan to release a Beta tomorrow-ish, and if that goes well the final client will be released around the weekend. This gives us roughly 3 weeks to bring everyone onto the new version. Watch here and the other channels for the announcements :)

-The Dogecoin CoreDevs"

On the 19th of August, a wallet client called "Dogecoin Core 1.8 beta 1" was released. It was released as a test for members of the community to use on testnet. Any flaws or bugs found could then be reported before the final release.

One day later at 03:11:43 UTC, user "CEX_IO" on Reddit notified Redditers that two trading pairs had been added to Cex.io. This was about three weeks after mining Dogecoin via the exchange's sister site GHASH.IO was made available:

> "Hey DOGE traders CEX.IO has added DOGE/BTC and DOGE/LTC trading pairs.
>
> Come and take a look.
>
> https://cex.io/#DOGE-BTC"

On the same day, funds which were being raised to help the ongoing development of Dogecoin surpassed 10 million DOGE. The developers praised everyone who had contributed. The funds would go towards the costs of testing the code.

Four days later, version 1.8 of the wallet client was released. Again, lead developer "langer_hans" at 18:00:46 UTC submitted an official announcement. It was mandatory for users to update as soon as possible before block number 371,337:

> "Hey shibes!
> It's done! Today we are here to release Dogecoin Core 1.8 as the final release. I will start with a TL;DR of the release notes. I'd recommend everyone reading them, especially if you are a service provider.
>
> ...(TECHNICAL DETAILS)...
>
> Again thanks to everyone who contributed to this release and also thanks to everyone who contributed to the dev fund!"

During the month, the lowest average recorded fiat value of one unit of DOGE account was reached for the entire first year. According to www.bitinfocharts.com, it was $0.00011 on the 18th of August.

MERGE MINING WITH LITECOIN BEGAN

SEPTEMBER 2014

I.   CheapAir.com began to accept Dogecoin as a method of payment.

II. At block number 371,337, merge mining with Litecoin started.

III. Doge4Kashmir target of 2.5 million DOGE successfully surpassed.

IV. From the start to the end of the month, value of one DOGE went up ~300%.

V.   "Follow The Coin" interviewed Jack Palmer (1st episode).

On the first day of the month, the Bitcoin Satoshi values of one unit of DOGE account equated to about $0.00013 in fiat terms. At the top of the next page, values from ten popular exchanges can be seen. Once again, the vast majority of trades with Bitcoin occurred on Cryptsy (nearly 71 BTC daily trading volume).

On the 3rd of September, it was reported that CheapAir.com had incorporated Dogecoin as a method of payment. Bitcoin was already an option for its customers. On the official CheapAir.com website, it describes Dogecoin as follows:

"Dogecoin is a super-cool digital currency (decentralized, peer-to-peer) that enables instant payments over the Internet. If you're already using Dogecoin, this is a simple alternative to paying with a credit card on CheapAir.com.
If you aren't aware of Dogecoin, maybe you should be – it's that awesome! If you've got some dogecoin to spend, we'll be happy to process your tickets this way, Shibe friends!"

	Price	Low	Open	Close	High	Volume (BTC)
Cryptsy	27.5	26	28	27	28	70.9762
Mintpal	27.5	26	27	28	28	8.12928
Bittrex	27	26	27	29	29	6.70864
Bter	27	26	27	27	28	5.77750
Vircurex	27.5	25	28	27	28	0.996068
Poloniex	28	26	27	29	29	0.789794
Bleutrade	27.5	26	26	29	29	0.326819
Kraken	27.5	27	28	27	29	0.118977
Swisscex	27.5	26	26	29	29	0.0350895
BTC38	27	27	27	27	27	0.00101571

source: www.cryptocoincharts.info

On the 11th of September, the switch to auxiliary proof of work kicked in. On the same day at 19:20:50 UTC, user "futile-resistance" said:

"Congrats on the successful fork. Massive increase in hashrate.

Join the Dogecoin IRC for the celebration, over 750 people on there atm."

As a consequence of the initiation of merge mining with Litecoin, the hash of the network protocol increased by a significant factor over the next few days. According to www.bitinfocharts.com, the average recorded hash was 67.06GHash/s on the 10th of September. Three days later, it had risen to 513.1GHash/s.

Block #371,337 (Reward 62,500) September 11th 2014 at 08:42:57 PM UTC

Also on the 11th of September, the community had successfully raised 2.5 million DOGE for flood relief in New Delhi and Lahore. Funds raised went to help purchase essential living and medical supplies. This campaign was called Doge4Kashmir:

"If you've been following the news, you've already heard about the devastation caused by the Kashmir floods in India and Pakistan. In what is being described as unprecedented in over 5 decades, the floods have left thousands homeless and over 400 dead across the two countries.

Communication lines are down in the flood-hit regions. Government aid has been promised but the main supply routes are cut off. We already have the national armies and private organisations engaging in relief efforts.

As part of Doge4Kashmir, we hope to raise 2.5 million dogecoins by Friday, 12th September 2014, closing the campaign at midnight PDT."

On the 17th of September, an update was posted on the official Dogecoin Foundation website titled "Such Wow, Many Work, Very Foundation". Since the beginning of July, progress had been slow to move the foundation towards where it wanted to be. Some of the major reasons why progress had been lacking were:

- Members of the board lacked time due to personal circumstances.

- Different time zones made communication between each other limited.

- Members of the board were being perfectionists (making sure things were being done properly)

Work had been done reviewing and incorporating all the feedback received on bylaws and compliance requirements. This would then determine how the foundation could then move forward in a legal sense.

Lack of communication had existed for some time concerning progress reports and getting people engaged. Members of the community were encouraged to help in relation to website development and to form a PR Team. A membership sign-up option for people who wanted to register to the foundation was also sought after.

On the 18th of September at 21:33:09 UTC, user "Brandon_Cryptonit" notified the community of the latest cryptocurrency exchange to add Dogecoin:

"Today BTC/DOGE pair was added at https://cryptonit.net exchange!

We enable trading today however DOGE deposits/withdrawals will be available from 24th of September 14:00 CEST

Thus everyone can get ready

Speaking about new altcoins, we have got our own Manifest to consider before to add some new coin to trade.
We beleive that DOGE is worth trading at Cryptonit because it is completely open source, was not premined, has strong enough hashing algorithm, DOGE developers have never offered us money for integration.
Our full manifest can be found here https://cryptonit.net/documentation/manifest"

Cryptonit is an exchange based in England and Wales. According to their official website, they have existed since 2012. At the time of publication of this book, very little trading volume of Dogecoin against Bitcoin occurs there.

On the 26th of September, a video titled "Hangout With Jackson Palmer, The DogeFather - Episode One: Epic Times in Crypto" was uploaded to YouTube by "Follow The Coin". Tina Hui, the founder and CEO of "Follow The Coin", asked Jack Palmer questions attaining to current Dogecoin events and other subjects related to cryptocurrency. Jack Palmer briefly described how he discovered Bitcoin, Litecoin and Feathercoin back in 2013. He also said he bought a jar ("big jar") of Nutella with DOGE as a reminder of cryptocurrency possessing value. At the end of the video, Jack brought up the possibility of creating a decentralised social network similar to Twitter. This is a project Jack was personally looking into.

On the last day of the month, the fiat price of one unit of DOGE account had risen by about 300% since the 1st of September. According to www.bitinfocharts.com, the average price was $0.00039 on this day. Statistics from ten exchanges were:

	Price	Low	Open	Close	High	Volume (BTC)
Cryptsy	104	100	104	104	106	711.727
Bter	104.5	99	104	105	107	77.2436
Mintpal	103	102	104	102	105	29.8887
Bittrex	103.5	100	104	103	106	19.0328
Poloniex	103	102	103	103	110	6.53681
Vircurex	104	100	106	102	107	5.83629
BTC38	106	102	107	105	107	3.35476
Kraken	103.5	103	104	103	106	2.76081
Bleutrade	103.5	102	104	103	111	1.64004
Swisscex	104	98	107	101	110	0.102424

source: www.cryptocoincharts.info

Other events which occurred in the month of September were:

- On the 15th of September, Dogecoin won the grand prize in the "Youth Citizen Entrepreneurship Competition" organised by the Goi Peace Foundation in Tokyo, Japan. To be exact, it topped the best ideas category with "Microlending with Dogecoin" in India.

- On the 16th of September, a mental health awareness campaign called Carlishio2 was initiated in order to help people battle depression . Carlishio had recently passed away and was part of the Dogecoin community early on. He was the creator of the funny Dogeball Comic Strip.

MAX KELLER INTERVIEWED AND TWO
ANNOUCEMENTS FROM THE FOUNDATION
OCTOBER 2014

I.   The fourth block reward halving occurred.

II.   Max Keller "langer_hans" interviewed by "The CoinFront".

III.   "Follow The Coin" interviewed Jack Palmer (2nd episode).

IV.   Twitch announced that they had accepted Dogecoin as a payment method.

V.   ZapChain interviewed Jack Palmer.

The conversation on the official Dogecoin Bitcointalk thread had now become slim. Over the next few months, each month had only a few pages of posts, comments or replies. As is the case today, the vast majority of discussion about the coin was happening on the Dogecoin Subreddit.

On the 2nd of October, the fourth block reward halving took place at block number 400,000 (see below). On average, a total of 45,000,000 DOGE would be mined each and every day until the next halving on the 14th of December 2014.

> Block #399,999 (Reward 62,500) October 2nd 2014 at 03:08:01 PM UTC

> Block #400,000 (Reward 31,250) October 2nd 2014 at 03:09:26 PM UTC

On the 4th of October, an article was written by Brad Edwards of "The CoinFront". Titled "Dogecoin Developer Langer Hans: "Very Moon, So Wow"", he interviewed the lead developer Max Keller ("langer_hans") to gain insight into how the Dogecoin community works behind the scenes (pages 147 to 153 of the appendix). Also on the 4th, an update from the Dogecoin Foundation was officially posted:

"Hi Shibes,

We hope everyone had a happy halvening and we'd like to share some news with you.

First off, we've uploaded the Foundation Bylaws and they are now available as PDF here.

We have successfully applied for an additional extension of two months for opposition of UltraPro's trademark registration of "Doge". The second extension was needed because we were close to the first extension deadline and research was still being done on similar cases and how best to approach it. We initially filed for the first extension at the last minute because there was no opposition recorded and, even though we were not prepared to file an opposition, we believed it was in the community's interests.

We are continuing to explore all avenues in regards to the trademark and have initiated talks with UltraPro to discuss several options, including those suggested by the community in their Q&A on /r/Dogecoin. So far, the communication with UltraPro is going smoothly. They have been very receptive and engaging.

To manage communication, we have appointed an interim Public Relations Officer, until an elected board can assign this function permanently. This should enable us to improve communications with the community and give you updates more often.

Last but not least, thanks to everyone who has been sending us emails offering support and assistance, we appreciate it! To get in touch with us directly, please email us at foundation@dogecoin.com."

Two days later, version 1.8.1 beta 1 of the wallet client was released. It was not a mandatory update. It introduced an integrated paper wallet generator. User "langer_hans" politely asked testers to report any code bugs on Reddit or github.

On the 8th of October at 21:32:04 UTC, user "futile-resistance" posted:

"For people who don't follow dogecoin on Reddit and Twitter, here's the second Dogecar:

http://thecoinfront.com/another-dogecar/

The Dogecoin subreddit has partially sponsored Australian V8 driver Jack Le Brocq, he'll be racing Dogecar II this weekend at Bathurst 250."

Three days later, Jack Le Brocq raced his V8 Supercar at the Supercheap Auto Bathurst 1000 event in Bathurst, New South Wales. He finished 10th out of 29 drivers (eight drivers retired during the race).

On the 12th of October, a video in which Tina Hui had another conversation with Jack Palmer was uploaded to YouTube. It was titled "Hangout Episode 2 With Jackson Palmer: Discussing BitLicense + Rumored SEC / FinCEN Crackdowns". They talked about upcoming regulations in cryptocurrency, especially Bitcoin.

Six days later, Josh Wise raced the Dogecar again at Talledega, Alabama in the United States. This time the car was not a Ford, but a Chevrolet. He finished the race in 28th position out of 43 racers.

On the 21st of October, a tweet was posted by @Twitch to announce that Dogecoin had been accepted as a means of payment on the live streaming video and gamers platform called Twitch. Twitch.tv was introduced in June 2011 and is owned by Twitch Interactive, a subsidiary of Amazon.com Inc. The following was tweeted:

> "We now accept DogeCoin! Just use the More Methods option when paying for a subscription. #FrankerZ"

On the following day, the second news post was published on the official Dogecoin Foundation website. It was titled "The Dogecoin Foundation comments on the NYDFS BitLicense":

> "Hello Shibes,
>
> Dogecoin sets itself apart from other digital currencies through its amazing, vibrant community made up of people from all walks of life.
>
> Our currency, which isn't even a year old, has brought us all together and has helped us achieve amazing and fun things: sending disadvantaged athletes to the Olympics, helping ones in need, seeing Doge's likeness whiz around the Talladega Speedway on national TV. One significant threat to the continued prosperity of digital currencies like Dogecoin and their immense potential for community building and action is the proposed NYDFS BitLicense regulation. In order to address this, the Dogecoin Foundation submitted comments to the NYDFS and its Superintendent, Benjamin Lawsky.
>
> In our comments, we focused on the potential for social good that digital currencies can unlock and offered our special perspective as a charitable non-profit organisation to aid them in their deliberations and to make sure that the interests of non-profits are served. We believe that a reasonable degree of regulation is key to the future success of digital currencies and welcome Superintendent Lawsky's inclusive approach and outreach towards the cryptocurrency community. We expect the NYDFS regulation to pave the way for regulation all around the world and if Lawsky continues his engagement with the community, then there is a good chance that the future will be bright for Dogecoin and other digital currencies."

A copy of their full comments to the NYDFS were made available at the time.

Other events which occurred in the month of October were:

- During the month, a Thunderclap campaign to raise awareness of Dogecoin's first birthday began. It is a platform used to broadcast a message through various social media sites. It lasted until the 8th of December 2014.

- On the 14th of October, a digital startup company called Moolah, said they would shut down at the end of the month. It had got to a point at which their operating costs were higher than their revenue. Moolah helped the Dogecoin community throughout some charity campaigns.

- A YouTube video was uploaded titled ""ZapChain Interview with Jackson Palmer, Creator of Dogecoin" on the 23rd of October. Jack answered some questions put forward by individuals. A few of these were "What is Dogecoin?", "How is "Doge" pronounced?" and "Is the future of Dogecoin in micropayments?". At the end of the video, he gave his thoughts about the Bitcoin community (https://www.youtube.com/watch?v=A3a6Bb_-w6E).

- On the 25th of October, users of the exchange mcxNOW were notified to withdraw all their DOGE before the 15th of November. They were going to remove all existing wallets to make way for a new system.

DOGEVERSARY EVENT ANNOUNCED

NOVEMBER 2014

On the 5th of November, the community were made aware of news regarding the Dogecoin TipBot. Led by Blackbird Ventures, a venture capital group based in Sydney, Australia, about $445,000 had been raised. There was interest in how cryptocurrencies could be leveraged to make micro transactions economically viable. Josh Mohland said the funding will be used over the next twelve months in order to develop the service further.

On the 11th of November, @ummjackson posted the following tweet:

"Announcing the Dogeversary on Dec 6 - register now! https://drive.google.com/file/d/0B0TFGRvmE4OQUUIyQ294UWI5aTQ/view ... #crypto #dogecoin #bitcoin #partyshibe"

Preparations were underway to organise this event so as to celebrate the success of the first year. The picture opposite was testimony to this.

On the 20th of November, Jack shared a platform with Tina Hui and Tim Swanson, Author of "Great Wall of Numbers", to discuss the future of cryptocurrency.

On the 29th of November, the Thunderclap campaign to broadcast the event of Dogecoin's first birthday had already surpassed its goal of 500 supporters. Also, a social reach of 675,666 people was achieved. Nine days still remained.

Only four pages of comments or replies were posted on the official Dogecoin Bitcointalk thread throughout the month.

DOGECOIN ONE YEAR ANNIVERSARY
DECEMBER 2014

I.   Josh Mohland wrote a personal article titled "On Tipping & Dogecoin".

II.   An exchange called Cryptopia began to trade Dogecoin.

III. Dogeversary conference in San Francisco occurred.

IV.   Last block of the first year was block number 491,142 at 03:54:38 UTC.

V.   First block of the second year was block number 491,143 at 03:58:09 UTC.

Seven days remained until the first anniversary of Dogecoin. An event had already been organised to celebrate this milestone called "Dogeversary" in San Francisco. There was no doubt that Dogecoin had made cryptocurrency less serious , more enjoyable and more friendly for the average member of the public.

Some charity campaigns that Dogecoin fund raised for over the last year were:

- Helping to send the Jamaican Bobsleigh Team to Sochi (dogesled).

- Helping to build two wells in Kenya ("Doge4Water").

- Sponsoring Nascar Driver Josh Wise ("Doge4Nascar").

- Helping to provide a free education to more than 750 Cambodian children.

- Helping flood victims in Kashmir ("Doge4Kashmir").

On the 5th of December, Josh Mohland wrote a personal article titled "On Tipping & Dogecoin". Since the 15th of December last year:

- Over 735,000 completed (accepted) tips had been processed.

- About 75,000 users had signed up to DogeTipBot.

- A mean transaction size of roughly $0.03 (60 DOGE) had been the case.

Towards the end of the article, he said:

> "2014 has been a crazy year for Dogecoin, but dogetipbot and Wow Such Business is just getting started. 2015 is definitely going to be our most fun year yet. We're extremely excited to make announcements as soon as our new products are done. :)"

One day later, the final exchange of the first year to add Dogecoin to their platform was called Cryptopia. At 01:35:34 UTC, user "TripleHeXXX" posted:

> "https://www.cryptopia.co.nz
>
> New Exchange, Mining Pool, and Buy/Sell/Auction."

Also on the 6th of December, the day of the "Dogeversary" event arrived. Jack Palmer opened proceedings by speaking about the initial history of the coin. A video message from Billy Markus was also shown. As was the case at the Dogecon conference back in April, Andreas Antonopoulo was the second person to speak.

On the 8th of December, user "C10H15N" was the first member to post on the official Dogecoin Bitcointalk thread regarding the coin's first birthday:

> "Happy 1st Birthday Dogecoin!
>
> With everything that has happened, I can't believe it has only been one year."

Originally created in October, the Thunderclap campaign to raise social awareness of Dogecoin's first birthday ended on the 8th of December. A total of 1,026,268 were reached and 900 people signed up to the campaign.

Also on the same day, an interview of Jackson Palmer was published. Anthony Cuthbertson of the International Business Times UK was the interviewer. A copy of the transcript can be found in the appendix of this book on pages 155 to 158.

The last block timestamped to the Dogechain during the first year happened at 03:54:38 UTC. A screenshot from www.bitinfocharts.com of this block is:

Number Of Transactions	8
Output Total	39,248,596.24305888 DOGE
Transaction Fees	7.07483437 DOGE
Height	491142
Time	2014-12-08 03:54:38
Mined by	/P2SH/
Difficulty	21,214.62858755
Bits	453187282
Size	2,303(bytes)
Version	6422786
Nonce	0
Block Reward	31,250 DOGE
Days Destroyed	341.159
Hash	5ad37ae6a60452a280c345bf4f8443833913d653e49076ec256d89be085fffa1
Previous Block	4858ee3a030ba096c133df9c7aa0426a2745c43da7440cb73a74085914c65415
Next Block(s)	24c62eb632248436ff03bfe5f020ca312ae22e728605f8058382a408d2b37d4c
Merkle Root	f38290786b60925c9887f93cba4da6fce15beb349308a40d22de4dfdecff6d4f

About three and half minutes later, the first block of the second year was found:

Block #491,143 (Reward 31,250) December 8th 2014 at 03:58:09 AM UTC

APPENDIX

PINGUINO INTERVIEWED BILLY MARKUS AND JACKSON PALMER PUBLISHED ON THE 14TH-15TH OF DECEMBER 2013

Where are you based out of and how did you meet?

Jackson: I'm based out of Sydney and Billy is based out of Oregon. Over the past few months I've been following cryptocurrency, so two weeks or so ago I posted a tweet along the lines of "Think I'm going to invest in Dogecoin #makeitrain". A couple of friends thought it was hilarious, so a few days later I Photoshopped the famous doge face onto a coin and through it up on dogecoin.com. At this point it was just a static site with the logo, and wasn't an actual currency yet.

Billy: I'm a Software Engineer from Portland, Oregon, and Jackson is a Marketing Guru Aussie, but I only knew that cos that's what it says on his Twitter! Basically we only met during the creation of this coin. It was my goal to create a coin that would get new people into cryptocurrency as I personally find it so fascinating, fun, and rewarding — but I didn't really have any great idea on what the coin should be. Fortunately for me, I stumbled across Jackson's brilliant idea of dogecoin at dogecoin.com from someone linking it in an IRC chat when it was just a splash screen and picture, and immediately thought two things: 1) "That is *hillarious*," and 2) "I have got to make this happen." So basically I tweeted at Jackson and started hacking away at it, and a few days later it was a reality!

How long did it take to develop after the initial concept? I've heard it's based on luckycoin- was there open source code that you just doge-ified?

Jackson: After dogecoin.com went live, it kind of went viral and tonnes of people were screaming for it to be made into an actual thing. That's when Billy contacted me via Twitter and told me he'd set up a QT Client for Windows. We synced up over email and launched it together a couple days later. From a technical standpoint, I'll let Billy comment there 🙂

Billy: Haha, I miss ONE string and everyone knows the secrets

The timeline was pretty quick. I tweeted at Jackson Thursday, finished the coin Saturday, then we released on Sunday.

Coin making (well, coin cloning), it does take quite a lot of initial time <u>investment</u> to learn the concepts and a decent amount of hacking away to setup your environments and dependencies and get compilation to work on various systems. But once you understand how that works, it's pretty straightforward, which is why there's so many of them! Get dependencies, git clone, change strings, change reward structure, change ports, generate merkle hash, create nodes, mine genesis block, customize the client, compile, and release! And then hope that people enjoy the effort, that part is actually quite nerve-wracking.

Did you expect it to garner so much attention so quickly?

Jackson: We initially thought it would just make the viral rounds on social media, attract a few miners for fun and then slow down. But something really interesting happened – it went from being a humorous take on cryptocurrency to actually <u>driving</u> mainstream awareness on the topic. People who'd never heard of or never used Bitcoin before we all of a sudden asking how to set up a Dogecoin wallet. For me, that's the best part of it, bringing something that was previously thought to be only for "nerds" into the public eye.

Billy: Haha, no, not at all! I was hoping people would appreciate the effort and enjoy the fun customized client and levity of the announcement post, but the way it has taken off is miles beyond anything I could reasonably expect. I've been absolutely thrilled with the reaction. I've actually never seen a coin grow so quickly, and in the cryptocoin world, everything moves ridiculously fast. I've described it as if I went and planted a single seed in the ground, then come back the next day to a fully grown forest.

The incredibly gratifying thing to me is how much community support we've gotten. People have told me they were impressed at how complete the launch was – we had pools and a subreddit and forums and games and a block explorer (a really well done one, too!) and IRC quite shortly after the release – but all me and Jackson did was make the client and webpage – a community just kind of blossomed from nowhere and did the rest. Mad props to @Drexme and the rest of the gang on doges.org for doing such an exceptional job, and everyone else who has contributed their time and efforts, you guys are the best <3

The other incredibly gratifying thing is seeing just how many people completely new to cryptocurrency are getting into DogeCoin. I think it could be a really good thing for cryptocurrency in general – a way for people to understand the concepts, how to mine, join pools, use the client, and trade – and really start getting into cryptocurrency and start checking out other intreguing coins and ideas that people are working on. It moves so incredibly fast and it's all so fascinating.

And finally I must say, the nonstop /g/ threads (especially http://i.imgur.com/xwgkYny.jpg) and pictures people are making (especially http://www.geek.com/wp-content/uploads/2013/12/dogegraphh.jpg) have been among the most amusing things I've ever seen. It's great to see so many people are having fun with it.

Are there any plans for the future of the coin or is it more of a fire and forget kind of idea?

Jackson: It's just currently the two of us, but we're looking to involve more people from the community in actively developing Dogecoin in the future. There's already a huge community building around it, with a sub-reddit, lively forums and a tonne of coverage online.

Billy: Well I'm committed on the dev side of the coin and Jackson on marketing, and the community is working on all sorts of things – see "DogeStarter", a take on KickStarter – http://doges.org/index.php?board=41.0 , there's a game in the works, an Android app, a Poker site, etc.

The thing I personally would love to see most, and that I hear is being developed, is a a tip bot for DogeCoin on reddit. I think people would be very generous with it and it would be exciting and fun for a lot of people. Lots of stuff going on, especially for a 6 day old coin!

What would you like to see people be able to buy with dogecoin?

Jackson: Anything and everything, ultimately. I think as "the fun cryptocurrency" it would be nice if sites such as 4chan, Reddit etc. somehow integrated it as a way of sending kudos or "tipping" somebody.

Billy: For one thing, I am a huge eSports fan, and today I saw that a Starcraft 2 ~tournament was being run with DogeCoins as the reward for winning, that completely made my day. I don't necessarily have pipe dreams that people would use DogeCoin to go to space or buy a car like they can with Bitcoin, but I love seeing it being exchanged for virtual goods like steam games and product keys (see http://doges.org/index.php?board=18.0) and given as prizes for contests and tournaments. I've also heard a few businesses have even started to accept it! I do hope to see the DogeCoin economy continue to grow and flourish.

Are you dog owners as well as fans of the meme?

Jackson: I don't currently own a dog unfortunately (renting, so not allowed!), but have had many in the past and love them.

Billy: Unfortunately no, I don't live in a place suitable for a dog. However, once I'm able to move to somewhere more suitable, I would LOVE to get a welsh corgi — and yes I admit it is all because of Ein in Cowboy Bebop. But I'd heavily consider a Shiba Inu now as well 😃

Are any developers working on a paper wallet or even a way to email it to a friend? It'd be really nice to give out dogecoin for Christmas.

Billy: They're already being made!

http://www.ebay.com/itm/1000-Physical-Dogecoins-High-Quality-Dogecoin-Paper-Wallet-/291037703040?hash=item43c332eb80

Do you think all the doge attention will anger the lolcat community?

Billy: Hehe well, I guess I have two things to say, one semi serious and one lighthearted —

My semi serious response is, I really hope that people don't see what happened with DogeCoin and try to make more popular-internet-memes into coins. I think a cryptocurrency based on a fun meme walks a really thin line between charming and obnoxious, and somehow the Doge meme is just so charming that it skillfully skirts that line and people can have a lot of fun with it. But I do think that if more get made like it, they could really start to become quite obnoxious and cross that line into negativity, and that would be sad to see given how positive things are right now.

But, in general for any dogs and cats argument, I would say both dogs and cats are plenty adorable and there's certainly plenty of room on the internet for both to amuse people!

How do you pronounce "dogecoin?"

Jackson: As for the pronunciation, I fluctuate between the "vogue" like pronunciation and "dohj" with a "j" sound ☺

Billy: Haha, usually I say "doDGe" and sometimes I say "Doh-ge". Either way is fun ☺

TWELVE QUESTIONS FOR JACKSON PALMER FROM THE DOGECOIN COMMUNITY 3RD OF JUNE 2014

1. "IS DOGE DEAD? WILL WE EVER GO TO THE MOON? DO WE HAVE A LEADERSHIP PROBLEM? WILL YOU COME BACK AND EVERYTHING WILL BE NORMAL AGAIN? WHAT IS GOING TO HAPPEN IN JANUARY 2015? AND WHAT CAN WE DO TO HELP?" – ASKED BYAMAOBATRON

Jackson Palmer, Creator of Dogecoin:

"Woh woh woh, that's a lot of questions 😛 Let me try and answer them all:

- Nope, only if you care about the BTC/USD price I guess

- Of course!!

Digital currencies shouldn't have centralized leadership, otherwise they're just as

open to corruption as our traditional fiat currencies right now... that being said,

some leader shibes from the community could help by stepping up and better

steering this ship

- I never left! 🙂

- In crypto, that's just too far out to predict. Bitcoin could be dead by then, for all we know... don't quote me on that, the press will have a field day haha"

2. "...I'M HOLDING A DOGECOIN HACKATHON IN JULY. ERIC IS ON BOARD ALONG WITH THE FOUNDER OF SOCHAIN! I WAS WONDERING IF YOU WANT IN (EITHER AS A JUDGE OR IN A GREATER CAPACITY!)" – ASKED BY SFDOGECOIN

Jackson:

"Hey hey! Hackathon sounds cool, I'd love to judge."

3. "HOW MANY [DOGECOINS] DO YOU OWN?" – ASKED BY XEDIVAD

Jackson:

"I didn't even mine Dogecoin when it first launched because I had an Nvidia card and couldn't get CudaMiner working. My co-founder Billy mined around 10mil in the first couple weeks or so and was kind enough to split that with me. 3mil of that has gone to things like charities, donations, tipping and I bought a few things with DOGE like coffee, video games, and a jar of nutella. I have roughly 2mil remaining, and I just emptied out my Dogetipbot wallet a couple days ago on mohland's awesome Reading Rainbow fund."

4. "ARE YOU AND BILLY COMING BACK TO US? WE MISS YOU ;D)" – ASKED BYGOODSHIBE

Jackson:

"We're still around, just not making all the decisions for the community. You can think free thoughts and do amazing things yourself :)"

5. "DO YOU HAPPEN TO BE A NASCAR OR V8 SUPERCARS FAN? AND WHAT DO YOU THINK OF THE FUNDRAISING WITH REGARDS TO THAT?" – ASKED BY MCANDZE

Jackson:

"I've been a little into V8 supercars, but admit that Josh Wise racing was my first foray into NASCAR. I enjoyed it and the Dogecar a lot ☺ It's kinda revolutionizing crowdfunding, right?"

6. "WAS DOGECOIN JUST A SPUR OF THE MOMENT TYPE OF THING, OR WAS THERE A PLAN BEFOREHAND TO MAKE A CRYPTOCURRENCY BUT PERHAPS JUST NOT WITH A DOGE ON IT?" – ASKED BY POLYANIMOUS

"I'd been into BTC/LTC/FTC a bit and literally went home one day, sat down with a beer and the word "Dogecoin" just popped into my head. So I tweeted about it. Now we're here :)"

7. "BEING THE MOST GENEROUS COIN IN DIGITAL CURRENCY ARE U PROUD BEING THE FOUNDER OF DOGECOIN? WHAT IS YOUR NEXT GOAL TO MAKE DOGECOIN BIGGER?" – ASKED BY HERI93

"My 'goal' has always been to just meet nice people and do great things together. Recently things went a little sour with all sorts of drama emerging from the community, but we have and continue to do amazing things with charities and community initiatives.

Also yes, I'm proud. But I see myself as just a regular shibe like you all :)"

8. "ARE YOU STILL TAKING INITIATIVES ON BEHALF OF DOGECOIN BY TALKING TO BUSINESSES AND HELPING OPEN THE DOOR TO OTHER OPPORTUNITIES? DECENTRALIZED OR NOT, OUR CURRENCY STILL HAS PUBLIC FACES AND, AS A CO-FOUNDER, YOU ARE ONE OF THEM. WE NEED YOU TO HELP IF YOU CAN." – ASKED BYREDSTARDAWN

"I'm meeting with a journalist this afternoon to speak about the history of Dogecoin and all the great things we've achieved over a coffee. So yes :)"

9. " HOW DOES IT FEEL BEING THE SPIRITUAL LEADER OF 87000 LUNATICS? DID YOU EVER ENVISION SOMETHING LIKE THAT FOR YOURSELF?" – ASKED BY CICEROTHEDOG

"Haha I've never heard it phrased that way… it's interesting? Although I don't see myself as a leader or in a position of power. If that's the case, it shouldn't be. We need to band together (every shibe) and make things happen. Strength in numbers."

10. "DO YOU STILL THINK THE PRICE OF DOGE DOES NOT MATTER AT ALL? WHEN IT WAS HIGH THE MOOD OF THE COMMUNITY WAS MUCH BETTER AND WE ACHIEVED A LOT OF COOL STUFF. NOW PEOPLE ARE JUST WINGING ABOUT THE PRICE DROP. NO MORE COOL FUND RISERS WITH A LOT OF IMPACT… ANY SMART IDEAS HOW TO GET BACK TO THE GOOD OLD DAYS? I MISS THE ENTHUSIASM WHICH SEEM TO BE CONNECTED TO THE PRICE, AT LEAST A BIT :-)" – ASKED BY GREENSIRIUS

"I'm a realist so I recognize that the price does matter to miners, unfortunately. This is one of the big flaws I take issue with in regards to all current-gen PoW-based cryptocurrencies – it pegs the security of the network to the fiat profit miners can reap by pointing their hashing power at that specific blockchain.

Once it becomes more expensive in USD to pay for that mining rig and the electricity it uses, the miners move to whatever is more profitable, and the overall hashrate of the network falls. The only reason this is more apparent with Dogecoin is because we accelerated the mining period with our short block times and reward schedule – Bitcoin, Litecoin and every other PoW coin is going to face this exact same predicament, albeit further down the line. I still think the future of digital currencies hinges on building awareness, acceptance and adoption from the mainstream group of internet users. I'm proud that Dogecoin has done the same, if not more than Bitcoin in promoting this type of growth."

11. "I APPRECIATE ALL OF THE DIRECTION YOU HAVE GIVEN THIS COIN/ MOVEMENT SO FAR, BUT WHY DOES IT SEEM NOW THAT THERE IS NO CLEAR DIRECTION? ALTHOUGH WE ARE DECENTRALIZED, THERE PROBABLY SHOULD BE A GROUP OF PEOPLE THAT PROVIDES DIRECTION FOR THIS COIN. YES, I READ ABOUT THE FOUNDATION IS GOING TO BE REFORMED, BUT WE NEED SOME DIRECTION TO GET THIS COIN TO BE MORE VALUABLE. EVEN IF 1 DOGE=1 DOGE, THAT MEANS NOTHING TO BUSINESSES AND MERCHANTS. ALSO, IF THE COIN HAS NO INTRINSIC VALUE (AS IS BECOMING NOW) IT WILL BE WORTHLESS FOR CHARITY EVENTS AND FUNDRAISERS. CAN YOU PLEASE COMMENT ON THIS?" – ASKED BY RESONANT1

"I've probably answered this in the bulk of my other comments indirectly, but I kind of agree that there needs to be stronger leaders within the community. My hope was that these leaders would emerge from the 80k+ shibes we have over here, and I still think they will with time.

As for 1 DOGE = 1 DOGE, that does mean something to businesses and merchants if they're able to then spend their earned Dogecoin on another business expense. It's about building an ecosystem of trade. You know what's worse than 1 DOGE = 1 DOGE? 1 BTC = \$US600... because all that it means for Bitcoin is that businesses/ merchants continue to care only about what Bitcoin means for them in the sense of USD revenue. They all cash out immediately rather than ever holding Bitcoin or believing in it's future as a store of value."

12. "WHERE DO YOU SEE YOURSELF FITTING INTO THE DOGECOIN ECOSPHERE? YOU CREATED A COIN WITH A DOG ON IT, BUT YOU DO NOT DO ANY OF THE CORE DEVELOPMENT. YOU ARE DOING TALKS ABOUT DOGECOIN / ATTENDING CONFERENCES, BUT YOU AREN'T PART OF ANY FOUNDATION-LIKE GROUP." – ASKED BY JESSTELFORD

"I see myself as continuing to help out advocating for Dogecoin and the use of digital currency in general. Some of the speaking I've been doing is more ~generalized and aimed at expanding the demographic of people getting into the use of digital currency.

One way or another, some of the big corporate giants like Apple, Facebook etc. are going to launch forms of tokens/credits/currencies in the near future as it's clearly what the online market is demanding – my hope is that by advocating and bringing about mainstream use of any cryptocurrency, we as a community of early digital currency adopters can keep the ball in our court, rather than having the bulk of the internet (who don't care about their privacy/security) switch to a new, centralized currency that's controlled by a corporation."

TRISTAN WINTERS OF BITCOIN MAGAZINE INTERVIEWED "LANGERHANS" PUBLISHED ON THE 30TH OF JULY 2014

What is your position in Dogecoin core development? How did you get into that position?

My position is lead developer. Basically this means I am responsible for advancing the development of the Dogecoin network and the Dogecoin Core reference client. Doing that I try to keep a balance between the management part of it and actually working on it myself. Lots of work is done by the team I am part of, for which I'm really thankful. The role was appointed to me already a few months ago by the founders of the coin. We got to know each other through reddit where I once pointed out a needed change for the client. From there I started working on it more and eventually I was made lead developer.

What is your training, experience and background?

I mainly work with Android, this is what caught my interest early on and is also what I do for a living. I did programming before as hobby and my education was mostly focused on CS. My experience with cryptocurrencies actually mainly comes from my work with Dogecoin, which I started by porting the Android wallet. I learned a lot while working on several Dogecoin related projects.

How many active contributors are there to the core Dogecoin code?

In the core development team, including me, we have currently four people from which three are the most active at this point of time. There is also the so called extended development team consisting of roughly 110 people. Not all of them contribute to the core client, but many are contributing either in code or in knowledge and advice.

What do you enjoy most about your work on Dogecoin core development?

If we are talking about the Dogecoin Core client, then it is the learning. As I said, I gained a lot of experience not only in programming, but also in managing the surrounding tasks of such an open source project – for example, managing the releases and the repository. If we extend it a bit further I also enjoy the community very much. It was what got me started with it and it is what keeps me going. I got to meet many nice people and found new friends which I greatly enjoy.

Dogecoin started life in jest, but it now has significant momentum behind it.With the rapid expansion of the community, brand and coin, also the hope, real investment and sunk costs, are you feeling the pressure?

Well, there is pressure, not only by service providers, but also the community. They all depend on a stable platform for their currency and their services. This is what we are trying to build and maintain and I think we did a good job with that so far. Our Core client is the most current one in terms of adoption of fixes from the Bitcoin codebase and we are overall very active developers. So yes, I can see the pressure, but it's not affecting me in a bad way.

Do you consider Dogecoin's recent declining hashrate a threat to the longevity of the coin? What proposals are currently on the table, if any, for addressing this issue? What, if any, is the time frame for implementing a solution?

A low hashrate is a threat for every Proof of Work based coin that doesn't implement special measures to mitigate possible attacks.

Dogecoin was brought to the market with an "expiration date" as the block reward schedule was made for about one year. That is basically the reason why we were already looking for solutions for quite some time.

The problem is that many of the solutions are either still highly theoretical or are deemed to be in an "Alpha" or "Beta" state. Some have technological issues, some have "political" issues. After the venture of Litecoin's creator into the Dogecoin subreddit, it seems that the implementation of the so called auxiliary proof of work is the most discussed one right now. While my recent reddit post about this may have seemingly implied differently, I'm not against this concept from the technical perspective. Yet, we still want to make sure that if this is considered to be the option to go with, there are no oversights of any concerns with it.

The Dogecoin community is passionate and active. After all the debate is done, who ultimately decides if any implementations or amendments to the coin are done? Who has the keys, so to speak?

We of course do continuously check what the community thinks. We then narrow it down through the development community to the core devs and ultimately it will be me as lead developer who "turns the key". That is also the reason why this seems to be such a lengthy process. [There are] many options to be considered and analyzed.

Do you consider a 51% attack an imminent threat? Is securing the network a primary concern of your team?

It is a threat yes, but I don't know the timescale in which it becomes feasible for an attack. The whole discussion currently happening is about the security of the coin. So yes, this is a primary, if not the primary concern.

Will Dogecoin merge mine with Litecoin?

I think the question is wrongly worded. The implementation of auxiliary proof of work does not mean "merging" the two coins.

It just happens that Litecoin is the coin with the highest hashrate on the scrypt algorithm. That means the Dogecoin network can accept blocks coming from their network, while securing it that way. Therefore I think the phrase "merged mining" is to be taken with a grain of salt.

Implementing AuxPoW is still on the table, yes. The decision will be made sooner rather than later. Then it will be about finding the time to implement the chosen solution.

Where do you see Dogecoin in 1 year and 5 years?

Alive & kickin' just like it did the last months. In one year I hope to see a stable currency that is is highly accepted and used by merchants and I still see the awesome community around it.

Five years is really hard to look forward to, as this is a whole lot of time in the cryptocurrency business. Every guess I'd take would be exactly that, just guessing. I do believe in Dogecoin and I hope to see it still around until then, maybe established as the currency of the internet which it aimed to become.

BRAD EDWARDS OF
THE COINFRONT
INTERVIEWED "LANGERHANS"
PUBLISHED ON THE
4TH OF OCTOBER 2014

I know you as Max, but the rest of the cryptocurrency world knows you as Langer Hans. Why did you choose this pseudonym?

The name? I used it long long before. There is actually no real story behind it. I found it funny many years back and stuck to it.

Well that's kind of anticlimactic

I know, people always expect a story behind it!

So what's your background? How did you first get into cryptocurrency?

I'm 24 years old, and an Android engineer and developer by day. I think if I remmeber correctly, I read about Bitcoin a few years back. I tried to mine with miserable success using a really low end GPU.

I came back when Litecoin was rallying around the $4 range and left pretty quick, cause I'm no economist and no trader. Then Dogecoin came up, which a friend of mine informed me of. I put it away as a funny thing but got back into it the day after. The cryptocurrency tech was interesting to me. Something new. So I stuck around.

What drew you to the cryptocurrency world in the first place?

What really drew me into it was Dogecoin!

I was looking for some new thing to take on as I had free time. Dogecoin and crypto in general was interesting because it was something new and innovative for me. I saw the opportunity to contribute to the community by developing. That being said, without the nice community, I'm not sure if I would have kept it up. So yes, the community played a big role actually. The ventures before, I wouldn't really call involvement.

When did you first get involved with Dogecoin?

Let me check...I received my first coins on December 11th. I heard about it the day before I think. It was a lot of reading first. Some chatting here and there, then I started actually working on things. The subreddit was created December 8th.

Cool, so you're a really early adopter. You've been there pretty much since the beginning. How do you see the community having developed? Is it still heading in a positive <u>direction</u> compared to the early days?

I feel like overall the community is still very positive. I enjoy what comes from it. I'd like to say that this also extends to the various other communities. It is a bit of a misconception that Dogecoin revolves around reddit. I also enjoy the IRC communities for example.

What do you think the IRC communities offer that /r/dogecoin doesn't?

Personally I'm a fan of realtime communication. It is fun. But comparing both is not really possible as they are very different concepts. The number of active users on IRC is actually most of the times higher than on reddit though.

You <u>recently implemented AuxPoW</u> to Dogecoin. Last time we talked, you mentioned there were some misconceptions about it. What are some of those?

First, it wasn't me who implemented it. It was lots of teamwork there to get it up and running from the core and the extended dev teams. And when it first came up, it looked to many like we would be actually "merging" with Litecoin. That is not correct though. Technically all that AuxPoW enables us is accepting work done on a different blockchain. Other coins would be able to supply the work too. Of course the hashrate now comes from Litecoin as they had it before.
The second one is, that AuxPoW is not a full protection against <u>51% attacks</u>, or any attacks for that matter. It just makes it harder (relative to the amount of hashrate put in and the distribution). Then, it was not first proposed by (Litecoin founder) Charlie Lee. It was brought up and had been discussed before.

Right, but it was Charlie Lee's proposal where most people first heard about AuxPoW right?

True, he was very vocal about it

Yeah, I remember the Dogecoinball comics about it portraying Litecoin as desperate for Dogecoin's love.

For the record, Charlie found the comics very funny and enjoyed them

I'd hope so. The Dogecoin community is too happy and friendly to be malicious about that sort of thing. So do you think AuxPoW is the reason for Dogecoin's recent surge in value?

That I'd opt to not comment on. Reason is that I'm a developer, and not an economist. It would be speculation either way.

Well do you think the price has much to do with Dogecoin's success?

Oh I think success of a coin comes from far more factors than just price. Adoption for example. Being actually useful in the real world.

Do you think Dogecoin is moving in the right direction in that regard?

It is one of the things to focus on. But yes, I think we did pretty good so far with adoption. I can for example buy a lot of things of all sorts with my coins. There are lots of service providers and merchants out there accepting Dogecoin. I can also use them tip on a high number of different platforms.

So you spend your dogecoins? What's the coolest thing you've bought with them so far?

I'm actually more into tipping and charity. I did look into buying stuff with it before. Mostly digital good like games. Nothing really outstanding there.

Speaking of charity, it's hard to argue that Dogecoin's charitable contributions have been Dogecoin's greatest victory from a community standpoint. Especially Josh Wise and the Dogecar. What do you think has been the greatest victory from a development standpoint?

From a development standpoint it was the move away from the Litecoin codebase to the Bitcoin codebase with version 1.7. We were actually the first altcoin who did that and are still the only one.

And for those of us who aren't familiar with code, what did that do for Dogecoin?

It brought us on par with the Bitcoin Core client. That includes the stability, the functionality and the development speed. We are now able to basically follow Bitcoin's development, thereby keeping up with the underlying tech that drives the network.
Giving us security and bug fixes along the way in a timely manner.

And that's more useful than being able to follow Litecoin?

There was not much following Litecoin. Dogecoin was brought to the latest Litecoin codebase with a previous version and after that we made the jump to Bitcoin, thereby implementing stuff that Litecoin didn't have at that point (mostly under the hood if I'm not mistaken at the moment).

What's the most difficult part of being a developer for Dogecoin?

I guess that's different from dev to dev. But I personally feel like it's the balance between working on the coin, the day job and free time. We're all volunteers.

And you've managed to accomplish so much so far. That's awesome.

Yup, the teams work very well.

Unlike most other cryptocurrencies, Dogecoin has no hard-coded limit. How do you think that will affect Dogecoin?

That pretty much would be looking into a crystal ball. It will be interesting to see how it develops overall. But estimations? Impossible to make. I'm not a fan of speculation. As I said, no background in economy things, so I don't want to burn my fingers there.

Other than Dogecoin, what do you think is the most interesting cryptocoin on the market right now?

I'm not looking at any specifically. I'm more looking in advancements in the technology itself. I think people call that Crypto 2.0. Personally I hold only Dogecoin at the moment.

Or let me correct that. I do have also Bitcoin, but not much. And may have received tips in other coins but not really worth mentioning.

So you're a one-coin guy, eh? Doge all the way?

It is what has drawn me into crypto and so far I stuck with it. Occasionally I got to help other coins, but that was mostly offering a hand for a moment or giving advice on dev related things. So pretty much one-coin-guy.

From a technical perspective, what do you think are the big issues the cryptocurrency needs to solve in order to move forward?

I think the user experience plays a key role in it. Crypto must be easy to use to gain higher mainstream usage. Usability is important. That of course extends to overall ease of use. Which is true for the other side, the services, too. The easier it is for a merchant to support crypto, the more likely it is for them to do it.

I think so too. Things are a little clunky right now, kind of like the early internet. But everything works better now that smart people have had a decade or two to make it easier

Agreed!

Now that AuxPoW is in place, what's next for the Dogecoin development team?

Immediate would be version 1.8.1 bringing us up par with Bitcoin again. It also introduces a new feature we'll talk about later on. After that we should have some time to also look a bit closer at the other wallet implementations like the light wallets out there, or even upcoming new projects. With a team of volunteers it's hard to set a fixed goal on things. But keeping up with Bitcoin definately plays a big role for us as a stable base of the network is very important to us too.

So you need to release an update every time Bitcoin does to keep up?

No, we don't need to. but it is what we are able to do. Of course, there will also be a delay, easily explained by the time we're able to put into it. If there is an immediate security issue though we'd be able to push things out faster.

So I know you're not a fan of speculation…but where would you like to see Dogecoin in the future?

I would love to see it as widely accepted currency and of course with the light hearted and fun community still around supporting wothwhile causes and having fun with tipping and using their coin. As I said above, acceptance is something to look forward to. So it would be great to see high adoption on both merchant/ services and user sides.

Well that's all the questions I had today Max. Thanks for taking the time to chat!

very moon. so wow

ANTHONY CUTHBERTSON OF THE IBTIMES UK INTERVIEWED JACK PALMER PUBLISHED ON THE 8TH OF DECEMBER 2014

IBTimes UK (IBT): Just over a year ago you joked about dogecoin, saying you were "pretty sure it's the next big thing". Was there any seriousness to this and could you ever have imagined how quickly it took off?

Jackson Palmer (JP): That initial tweet was really a jab at the Bitcoin and altcoin scene at the time - I noticed that SomethingCoin was popping up every couple of weeks (it's even more prevalent now) and wrote that tweet on a whim. A few of my friends latched onto the idea and my co-founder Billy reached out with the first official build of the Qt client... so I purchased Dogecoin.com, put up a basic website and the rest is history.

IBT: Why the Shiba Inu?

JP: I'd always loved the doge meme (the infamous photoset of Kabosu, celebrity Shiba Inu) and had just read an article by Adrian Chen about it actually being a good meme. Combined with my interest in cryptocurrency at the time, I put the two together and laughed to myself. Thankfully I decided to share my personal joke with the world.

IBT: What has most surprised you about dogecoin and its community? Is there one particular event or campaign that you're particularly proud of?

JP: I'd say the most impactful event was raising the $30k to help send the Jamaican bobsled team to the Winter Olympics. That all happened in around 24 hours and was something I'd never done before, nor would ever have imagined doing. That was the first point at which I really saw the sheer power of this community and realized that Dogecoin was here to stay.

IBT: Has there been any real low points over the last 12 months (Trademark disputes/ 'Alex Green' fiasco, etc.)?

JP: The trademark dispute was always a non-starter for me, because I simply called up Ultra Pro (the company seeking the "doge" trademark to legally protect themselves) and realised there was no malicious intent. Making such a big deal of it was more a PR stunt by Moolah in my mind.

On the topic of Moolah, I'd say that's <u>the biggest low we faced over the past 12 months</u>. Ben Doernberg and myself had raised concerns that were ignored several times earlier in the year about this company, and it's really sad as the founder of something to watch your community march towards what you know is disaster. In typical Dogecoin fashion, I think the community has bounced back though... and if anything a lot of folks learned a lesson in exercising healthy skepticism, especially when it comes to the crypto world.

IBT: Do you think that given dogecoin's overall success, combined with its recent run of stability, that dogecoin is being taken seriously by both those within the community and the wider <u>financial</u> world?

I've never really promoted Dogecoin as the "fiat killer" like Bitcoin and it's community like to prophecise. Dogecoin is a really fun, absurd community and a currency that people use to throw change at each other on the internet in the <u>form</u> of micro-tips. It's also a great education tool and awareness builder for Bitcoin and digital currency as a movement, which I think is great. Is Dogecoin ever going to rock the foundations of the financial world? No, and that was never it's intent. The second people forget that and start taking Dogecoin too seriously is the

IBT: How much involvement do you still have with dogecoin and its development?

JP: I'm still quite involved in the community side of things, speaking at conferences and trying my hardest to keep things fun. As long as the community continues to value my thoughts and wants me to help steer the future of Dogecoin, I'll always be here for them. As far as development goes, there is a team of volunteers who maintain the codebase and are far more qualified to do so than I ever was. There is also a passionate team behind the Dogecoin Foundation who are helping with outreach, legal issues etc.

IBT: As the creator of this 'joke currency' that once had a market cap of more than $90 million (currently $20m), have you personally made a small fortune from dogecoin?

JP: Lots of people assume this, but absolutely not. Billy and I only ever had around 5 -6 million Dogecoin each (I didn't get my miner set up fast enough because I had an Nvidia card), which at the price peak was still only worth a few thousand USD. The bulk of the Dogecoin I did have has gone towards charity drives and tipping over the past 12 months. I did buy a jar of massive Nutella with my doge, which sits on my desk at work.

IBT: Finally, getting out your crystal ball, what do you think the future holds for dogecoin?

JP: There is no way to predict the world of crypto, I've learned. At the end of the day, the community of users behind Dogecoin are going to define this future.In my eyes, if they never lose sight of the fact that Dogecoin is supposed to be fun, inclusive and at it's core hilarious then it's a future I'm going to stick around for.

www.ingramcontent.com/pod-product-compliance
Lightning Source LLC
Chambersburg PA
CBHW051214170526
45166CB00005B/1893